Animals Nobody Loves

Animals Nobody Loves

By Ronald Rood

Illustrated by Russ W. Buzzell

The Stephen Greene Press

Brattleboro, Vermont

To Mrs. Ruby S. North—the patient schoolmarm who suffered through so many of my turtles and frogs—this book is affectionately dedicated.

And God made the beast of the earth after his kind, and cattle after their kind, and every thing that creepeth upon the earth after his kind: and God saw that it was good.

GENESIS 1:25

The author and publisher are grateful for permission to quote material from *Cannery Row* by John Steinbeck. Copyright, 1945, by John Steinbeck. All rights reserved. Reprinted by permission of The Viking Press, Inc., New York. And material from *A Naturalist in Alaska* by Adolph Murie. Copyright © 1963 by Adolph Murie. Published by Devin Adair Company, New York.

Portions of the following material appeared in different form in the publications noted, to whom the author expresses his gratitude for permission to reprint: "Flea" from *Audubon* Magazine, forthcoming; "Mosquito" from *Pageant* Magazine, © July 1969, *Pageant;* "Snake" from *Vermont Life* Magazine, © Autumn 1967, *Vermont Life.*

Copyright © 1971 by Ronald Rood

This book has been produced in the United States of America: designed by R. L. Dothard Associates, printed and bound by Halliday Lithograph Corporation.

It is published by The Stephen Greene Press, Brattleboro, Vermont 05301.

Library of Congress Catalog Card Number: 70-118222

International Standard Book Number: 0-8289-0128-7

Contents

ALSO BY RONALD ROOD

Wild Brother
Hundred Acre Welcome
Vermont Life Book of Nature
How Do You Spank a Porcupine?
The Loon in My Bathtub
Land Alive

JUVENILE BOOKS

How and Why Book of Ants and Bees
How and Why Book of Butterflies and Moths
How and Why Book of Insects
Wonder Book of Insects We Know
Bees, Bugs and Beetles
The Sea and Its Wonderful Creatures
Animal Champions

With a Little Understanding

HER yellow eyes gazed at me, unblinking. Her wing drooped uselessly, and she kept settling down on her left leg as if it was too weak to bear the weight of her body.

"All right," I said. "A dollar."

"Nope," said the man, shutting the cardboard carton. He sensed that I wanted this red-shouldered hawk, and he was determined to make the most of it. "Three."

"Two," I countered.

"Two-fifty."

It made my blood boil to be thus haggling over the life of a wounded hawk. He had brought her to me in his car, and his story was that the bird was "nothing but an old chicken hawk."

"I got in a lucky shot while it was circling over my farm yesterday," he said. "It hit the ground like a ton of bricks, but I think I just winged it. What's a chicken hawk worth to you, Mr. Rood?"

Maybe if I got my hands on her I could nurse her back to health. It was at this point that the bargaining had begun.

"Two dollars," I repeated. "You can't tell how bad it's hurt. How do you know it'll even live? Besides, I'm meeting you halfway."

He shrugged. "I suppose so. Okay—for two bucks it's yours."

It would have done no good, of course, to lecture him on

1

the folly of blasting away at the best living rat-trap his farm ever had. He already knew hawks were protected by law in Vermont—as they are in most states. If I had adopted a righteous attitude he would merely have driven away with the doomed bird.

So I found the two dollars and swapped it for the hawk. I wish now that I had paid him by check, with the notation "Blood money for one hawk illegally shot." But you don't think of those things at the time.

The man's trouble was not really an itchy trigger finger. He just could not understand where a high-flying hawk fitted into the scheme of things on his farm. Any large, soaring bird was a "chicken hawk," even though no such creature actually exists. Lacking any clear evidence as to how the hawk could possibly benefit him, he took what seemed to him the logical course: *Get rid of it.*

Not everybody feels this way about hawks. And, if you get right down to it, there is probably not one animal that isn't liked by somebody. Few people think kindly of a sloth, for instance; if a person is slothful, he's about as useless as he can be. Yet Hermann Tirler's heartwarming *A Sloth in the Family* gives a whole new view of this misunderstood creature.

In my own case there was a time when I couldn't think of much to say for porcupines. They chewed the bark of our trees and cut the Vermont sugarmaker's newfangled plastic tubing as it ran from the maples. They raised general havoc where sweaty hands had touched any article and left a tasty film of salt. One of them also liberally punctured our dog, who had to be de-stickered by a veterinarian.

This was how things were before we had our own porcupine. We stumbled across a newborn orphan porky in our woods. After bringing him home for what turned out to be a year's stay, we learned one thing about the quill-pig: he can be perfectly delightful.

2

This human tendency to label everything as "good" or "bad" goes with us all through life. I taught biology for several years, and one of the favorite questions of my students on encountering a new animal was, "What good is it?" Sometimes I was hard put for an answer. Although I had taught them that nothing in nature is entirely useless, and each thing has its place, they still wondered just where that place might be. What on earth was the use of a mosquito? Or a fly? Or a cobra?

To delve into the "use" of every animal would be impossible—especially if we started with that ecological misfit, man. Yet the matter arises again and again.

If the answer to the question is not just right, the animal suffers. I worked with the New York State Extension Service for several years, answering letters and receiving visitors from all over Long Island and the metropolitan New York area. Over and over, people would bring me an insect or perhaps a shrew, mouse, snake or even a bird—all very dead. When I asked how the creature died, the same answer came forth so often that I even chanted it with them once or twice in exasperation: "I didn't know what it was, so I killed it."

Thus apparently human beings don't actually have to hate particular animals—we just have to misunderstand them a little.

One day I was having coffee with my publisher, Stephen Greene, and Arthur Burrows, his managing editor. I told them about the hawk—who died in my hands the night I got it, by the way—and all the trouble that befalls living things because we don't take the trouble to know them better.

"Andy" Burrows warmed to the subject at once. "There are books written about raccoons," he said, "and bear cubs and rabbits. Take any cute little animal and chances are somebody's written a book about it. But how about the ones on the other side of the fence—the animals nobody loves? Why not tell *their* story?"

People have used particular animals symbolically and epithetically, Andy said, and it's not fair to the animals. A wolf is a love-'em-and-leave-'em heel; a little rat is a sneaky coward; a pig is a glutton with filthy habits; an octopus is a predatory enveloper of undersea explorers. And so on, and on.

And what, continued Andy, made human beings decide to hate them all in the first place?

He had something there. As we discussed it, it seemed to me that men have taken a scunner against certain species because of three main reasons: the way the creatures act (or at least the way we think they act); the way they look; and a combination of actions and appearance.

After more talk, we decided that someone should tell the animals' side of the story. And so, eventually, came this book.

You will find here the life histories of just a few of the creatures that have had more than their share of man's maledictions, that have been hunted and harassed, repulsed and rejected. If you do not agree with our choices, you can probably go us one—or two, or more—better.

In which case you'll be lending a hand to helping the cause of animals who could do with a little understanding—maybe even a little love.

The Way

They Act

Wolf

The wolf is naturally dull and cowardly. The color of the eyeballs is of a fiery green. *Wonders of the World,* 1894

There is nothing valuable about wolves except their skins. They are such ferocious and useless creatures that all other animals detest them—yea, they even hate each other. They are particularly fond of human flesh, and perhaps, if they were sufficiently powerful, would eat no other.
Natural History (American Sunday School Union), 1827

OUR little seaplane banked in a slow turn. Behind us was the end of Michigan's Upper Peninsula. Beneath us sparkled some sixty miles of Lake Superior. And before us, just off the left wing, stretched one of the most fascinating places in North America.

The maps show it merely as Isle Royale National Park. For us, however, it held a special meaning. This bit of land poking up through those wonderfully clear waters is the home of one of the animals most respected by those who know him —and most feared by those who don't: the North American timber wolf.

You can read in travel guides that Isle Royale, Michigan, is forty-five miles of ridges laid in parallel bands ranging up to nine miles in total width. You can see photographs of the herons, squirrels, loons, beaver and ravens which make this quiet land their home. Postcards show the boat facilities in its sheltered harbors. National Park pamphlets guide you to the campsites at several points on the island. The pamphlets and cards often show pictures of the lofty moose which browse on the foliage and, in the brief summer, wade in the shallows for edible water plants.

But you seldom hear a word about the timber wolf. Thousands of vacationists come and go during the camping season with no mention of his name. I'm sure many of them would flee with the galloping shudders if they knew he even lived on the island.

For wolves, after all, are painted as the very incarnation of evil. They pursue terrified horsemen through the black of night at headlong speed. They come slavering to the edge of remote northern villages the world over, jumping and snarling as the desperate housewife puts all her strength against the door from within. They cut the shepherd's faithful dog to ribbons and slaughter the sheep before his horrified eyes.

There's only one thing for believers in such tales to do with a creature so fearsome: destroy it wherever it is found. Over almost all of its range in North America and Eurasia, the timber wolf has been a hunted animal for centuries. Rare, indeed, have been the persons who have risen to its defense. Although wolves now exist in the Western Hemisphere in only a few little pockets of wilderness in the United States and Canada, even these last strongholds will soon be gone. Just the hint of the presence of a solitary wolf brings forth men with their guns to do him in. And when the chase is successful, there are not only the envious stares of his fellow men to reward the hunter, but in many cases he'll even receive a bounty check from a grateful local government for his deed.

Very little is said about the other side of the coin. We seldom hear of the loyalty that may lead this great wild dog to face the executioner along with his trapped mate. We know little of the chivalry that prompts him to grant mercy to a vanquished rival, or the family ties that call the female to face a hail of bullets to rescue a tethered pup. These facets of a wolf's personality are conveniently forgotten—if, indeed, they are ever known at all. In our enlightened United States and Canada there is only the license to hunt; there is no license whatever to allow to live.

Above all, the wolf isn't supposed to be anywhere near a vacationer's campfire. Mother should be able to fry Daddy's fish while Junior toddles off into the bushes after a butterfly. This all should happen with no thought that the ravening beast might be within a day's journey.

Just the same, he's there. Out beyond the glow of the fire and back away from the trails he digs his den and raises his pups. During the winter, when the island rarely hears the sound of a human voice, he lifts his muzzle in a mournful howl. In the summer, his howls and his barks—for wolves do bark—are back in the interior wilds of the island. Here the shy wolf finds his living far beyond the few hiking paths with their (to him) noisy, smelly people.

I had heard wolves howl in Alaska years ago. Two college friends and I were there on an after-graduation jaunt just a few months before Pearl Harbor. Out in those lonesome wilds the wolf cries served only to deepen the silence. Perhaps, sometime during those few days on Isle Royale, I might hear them once again.

We had timed our visit to arrive shortly after the winter snows had left. We wanted to be there before the rugged grandeur of the island lured the annual influx of campers, for whom the very isolation of the place presented a challenge. If luck favored us, we might even catch a glimpse of old Lobo. After all, he had padded through the woods unmolested for half a year now since the last hamburger had been barbecued. Perhaps the respite had dulled his natural caution. Stephen Greene and I hoped so, at least. Steve is my publisher and shares my love of the outdoors.

There was more to this trip than just curiosity, however. Back in the early 1940's I'd been interested in Isle Royale. Surrounded by fifteen to sixty miles of deep water—the distances to Canada and Michigan, respectively—the island is a little world in itself. Birds visit it regularly, of course, and many insects can make the round trip to the mainland by air. The larger animals find the voyage much more difficult. To all purposes they must live forever in harmony with their neighbors on this sliver of land. If they can't get along, they'll die out.

The wilderness island became a National Park in 1940. In so doing, farseeing conservationists prevented the partitioning and development that might well have taken place in a few years. Thus the plants and animals could work out their destiny here, much as they had for eons before man came on the scene.

This living laboratory, isolated by the moat of Lake Superior, has intrigued biologists for years. They've studied it on tiptoe, as it were, to learn as much as they could without disturbing its fragile balance of nature. And it was for this reason that we were there too: to travel alone in its stillness, discovering what we could about its plants and animals—and, especially, those wolves.

Our pilot brought the Cessna in for a landing on a quiet

10

bay. The Park headquarters in Houghton, some seventy miles back on the Michigan mainland, had radioed ahead. Now we were met by Robert Rogers, Chief Park Ranger.

"Got just the spot for you," he grinned. "Couple of miles from here. Daisy Farm campsite. If you really want to be alone, that's the place. One of our boats is going past there; they'll drop you off."

An hour later we stood on the dock of Daisy Farm—that narrow strip of shore so crowded with tourists in summer, but so quiet on this day in May. We watched the departing motorboat, then turned to make camp.

We'd scarcely settled down in one of the little lean-to's before the sound of an outboard motor brought us back to the water's edge. A young man with a winter's growth of whiskers stepped out of the little boat.

"I'm Mike Wolfe," he said, extending his hand. "The office told me you were doing a story on the wolves. I've been doing post-doctoral work on them, myself."

He tilted his head toward a cabin across the inlet. "How about coming over for a cup of coffee?"

Thus Steve and I met Dr. Michael Wolfe, superb naturalist and a former Fulbright scholar. In my correspondence with the Park officials, I had learned of Mike and his interest in the wolves of the island; now I had the chance to meet Marie-luise, his wife, plus Mike Kochert, the graduate student who was helping him collect data. Sitting in the circle of light cast by a gasoline lantern, we talked far into the night, reviewing the facts of the well-nigh incredible story of the wolves and the moose.

Part of our misunderstanding of the wolf is that we are not clear as to just exactly how it fits into the lives of other animals. It's not as simple as "wolf catches prey; the more wolves, the fewer prey animals will be left." Things are far more delicate than that—immeasurably, wonderfully, so. And

11

the story of Isle Royale shows how the wolf can actually be the best friend the moose has ever had. Hence to present this predator in his true light it may be helpful first to follow the fortunes of his gigantic prey.

Nobody knows how the first moose may have made its appearance on the island. A 1905 census of all its animals makes no mention of this largest member of the deer family. But at some point since then, a moose or two may have crossed the winter ice from the Canadian shore. More likely the moose, a strong swimmer, may have made the fifteen-mile trip by swimming. Probably such piecemeal migration took place on several occasions.

No matter, though, how it happened; suddenly there were moose on Isle Royale. They found things very much to their liking: plenty of young, succulent browse along the shoreline of the bays and inlets, and plenty of sheltered spots in which to have their calves. Furthermore, there were no enemies. No grizzly bears, no cougars and, at that time, no wolves. Even the human beings, represented by a few loggers, copper miners and fishermen, scarcely bothered them.

By World War I there were an estimated three hundred moose on the island. As they multiplied they had to look farther for food; the youngsters, growing to maturity, were forced to find new territory for themselves. They moved to less desirable parts of the island. There, following their natural urges, they bred and produced more calves—which, in turn, produced still more.

By 1921 there were perhaps a thousand moose on the island. Food was hard to find now, but still they multiplied. By 1926 their numbers had doubled.

Now things were serious. With scarcely more than two hundred square miles to the whole island and all its little islets, there was an average of ten moose per square mile. The good low-growing browse had long since been eaten; now the desperate animals had to reach higher into the trees. They straddled and "rode down" smaller trees for the last bit of browse.

Winter was the worst time. With snow thick on the ground, and ice covering succulent water plants that might have remained from the summer, the moose were in desperate straits. A telltale sign of overcrowding appeared in the forest: The "browse line," where the animals had completely removed any edible lower branches from thousands of acres of trees, had made the bottom ten feet of woodland almost like a city park. Tree trunks were growing up nakedly, bearing scarcely a limb until the twigs and branches were out of reach. Even the bark was stripped from the trunks—and of course if the trees were completely girdled they died.

As we talked, Mike described suffering moose that had been seen in those bad days by Pete Edisen, a veteran fisherman who had spent years on the island. Later, when we met Pete and his wife, Laura, I questioned him about the unfortunate animals.

The dead moose, according to Pete, could be found lying with half their hair missing and their bones almost poking out through their skins. When he opened their stomachs he found chunks of bark, tree roots, and coarse twigs as big as a man's thumb. "Anything to fill that hungry stomach," Pete recalled.

So the tragic situation continued. Starving females plodded through the woods, followed by starving calves. Young and old, somehow eking it out through the summer, died in the winter snow. Yet the losses could not catch up to the birth rate. By the 1930's there may have been as many as four thousand of the hapless animals crowded together on the island.

The crash came in the late 1930's. The animals died by the hundreds. By 1938 there were only an estimated five hundred moose on the island. Yet even this remnant faced the same bitter fate.

A fire in 1936, which burned the trees on nearly a quarter of the island, turned out to be a blessing, as young edible browse sprang up in its wake. But the blessing would be only temporary. The exhausted land, still reeling from the enormous demands it had suffered, could never support the same dreadful build-up again.

Then came the timber wolf. How it actually got there is as much a mystery as the arrival of the moose, for wolves are great wanderers and they can cover more than twenty miles in a night. Perhaps a few of them crossed the winter ice from Canada. Be that as it may, in 1948 the evidence was clear: there were wolves on the island.

The big, wild cousins of our familiar household pets made themselves right at home. And they, too, began to multiply.

The wolf is intensely loyal to his family, and parents and young may all travel together in a pack as soon as the cubs are old enough to keep up with the adults. There may be several relatives along, as well. Where possible the wolves caught a snowshoe hare or a beaver. But a forty-pound beaver doesn't go very far when you're feeding all the kinfolks—even if you clean up every scrap in typical wolf style. Thus the wolves looked for more sizable prey.

This is where the moose came in. True, a belligerent, healthy adult moose is too formidable for even a pack of wolves, but a weaker animal may be another story. So is a moose calf, if its mother is slow to protect it.

Now began a new chapter for the moose. Starvation-weakened individuals were spared the long ordeal of grinding hunger by the swift attention of the wolves. If a cow was sickly and unable to care for her young, both might be caught and killed. The alert, healthy animals thus were spared. With typical canine thrift the wolves made good use of the entire carcass of the weaker ones. They even ate part of the hide, gnawed the hoofs and cracked the bones for the marrow.

14

I had long known of the "sanitary value" of predators in weeding out the unfit. When I first heard of Isle Royale the wolves had not yet arrived and the moose were having it the hardest. The introduction of wolves had been suggested at the time; now it has been a fact for more than twenty years.

Dr. Durward L. Allen, the famous biologist and writer, had for years been interested in the relationship between hunter and hunted, and the wolves and moose of Isle Royale seemed made to order for his studies. In 1958 Dr. Allen began the investigation which continues as a study project under the auspices of Purdue University. His doctoral student, L. David Mech, followed with the fascinating *Wolves of Isle Royale*, published in 1966 by the National Park Service and, more recently, with *The Wolf*. Now, following Mech, and in a joint project supported by the National Science Foundation and National Park Service, Dr. Michael Wolfe continues to add to the priceless data on the fabled animal and its huge prey.

"It's hard to say what goes on in summer," Mike Wolfe admitted. "With the campers and hikers all over, and foliage covering everything, we seldom really know what's happening. But it's different in winter. The wolves and moose show up dark against the snow. And they leave tracks.

"We fly airplane surveys in the winter," he continued. "When a moose gets killed, we mark the spot on a map. Then we hike to the area in the spring—or winter, if we can—and try to determine the condition of the moose when it was killed. This, we hope, will tell us why the wolves were able to catch it."

He unrolled a large map of the island. It showed the ridges with their lakes and fjords, all running from southwest to northeast. "Right here's where a pack of wolves killed a moose last February. We're hiking to the spot tomorrow. Want to come along?"

Did we? Even though we had planned our visit with them for months, this was an unexpected bonus. The most we'd dared hope for was a chance to talk with Mike and with some of those National Park employees who lived in this self-contained little world. Plus, of course, that outside chance that we'd hear the howl of a wolf. But to walk through the woods with a team of naturalists to the very spot where those elusive wolves had downed a moose—this was rare, indeed. Did we want to go? Does a duck like to swim?

After we had finished our plans for the next day Mike took us back across the bay. He had regaled us with so many stories of wolves that we half expected shadowy forms to go dashing away from our darkened campsite. But our flashlights picked up the gleam of only one set of eyes—the tiny glittering orbs of a single moth as it circled in the cold air.

I lay in the sleeping bag, pondering the rare good fortune which allowed me to spend the night in this Michigan wilderness. As I tried to set my mental alarm clock to awaken early, a long, quavery cry came to me on the night air. I tried to make it into the call of a wolf but, wild as it was, it remained no more—and no less—than the lonely laughter of a loon out there on the dark water.

The loon called again. Now, instead of sounding far away, its voice seemed to be just outside the cabin. I woke with a start. Daylight.

The loon was, indeed, just outside. As I jumped to my feet the great bird flew over, long neck outstretched and powerful wings driving him swiftly out over the water. He was at treetop level, and his white breast glowed orange in the sunrise.

A grunt of despair from the cabin told me that Steve had heard the loon, too. He'd extricated his six-foot-four length from the sleeping bag and was fumbling with his camera. But the loon wouldn't oblige by circling back. Instead our

16

flying alarm clock flew off down the shore against a backdrop of evergreens, poplar and birch.

The world was alive that May morning. A raven drifted over a large spruce tree and fled, croaking, when half a dozen crows rose to meet him. The spruce probably contained a nest of one of the crows. From the indignant outcry of those black rascals, you'd think they suspected the intentions of their large cousin. And they ought to know: crows are confirmed nest robbers themselves.

There were other sounds—warblers singing their way north; a Wilson's thrush, or veery, echoing its liquid note as from the depths of a long pipe; flickers and woodpeckers hammering and calling; the chattering of a red squirrel in a fir tree; ducks quacking out on the lake. Steve and I made our breakfast to the sound of perhaps a hundred birds.

An hour later, after a boat ride up the bay, we set out on a well-marked trail. The five of us must have made an interesting sight: white-haired Steve striding along in front; red-bearded Mike Wolfe behind him; be-mustached Mike Kochert next; then sandy-haired Larry Roop, who was also studying wolves and moose; and Ron Rood, resplendent in thinning gray-brown hair, bringing up the rear. And, since the weather was cool, each of us sported his own version of a colorful hiking jacket.

I started out just behind Steve, by the way, but every few steps I would pause to look at some plant, or to marvel at a piece of rock. I soon became Tail-end Charlie, but Larry made it his special business to stick with me. Patiently he would nudge a wildflower into a patch of sunlight for a photograph, or be suitably impressed when I exclaimed over some bit of local scenery.

We came upon our first moose so suddenly that none of us had a chance to warn the others. One moment the trail had been dark and quiet ahead; the next, it was bathed in sunlight.

In a flash we realized the "darkness" hadn't been what we'd thought at all, but the broad expanse of a great bull moose, half hidden by the leaves. The sunlight had appeared when the moose moved away.

Although we were "frozen" only thirty feet distant, the wind was in our favor. The bull neither smelled nor heard us. But he realized something was amiss. Standing there, partly concealed by a poplar, he sniffed the air. We could see the nubbins of his developing antlers and the "bell" of flesh and hair hanging beneath his chin. Those great sound-scoop ears swiveled slowly, trying to catch the faintest noise.

The breeze faltered. Then it must have eddied around between us and the moose. And there was no mistaking the instant when he got our scent. Jumping back as if he'd been struck on the nose, he whirled and ran.

Not a panicky, headlong flight—after all, this was a bull moose. Indeed, if it had been rutting season, he might have charged. Or he might even have circled around and stalked us from behind, as one did to Larry last fall (Larry took refuge in a tree just inches ahead of the bellicose animal). As it was, however, this moose retreated in a long-legged, ground-covering, effortless trot. In a moment he was gone.

We relaxed. Then Larry chuckled. "How'd you like to be a wolf and have to catch something like *that* for your daily bread?"

I considered what we had seen. Naturally the wolves know better than to attack a thousand pounds of healthy moose. The antlers aren't so much to be feared—they're borne only by the males in fall and early winter and used mainly for battle with other males—but the hoofs of a moose of either sex are murderous. One blow of any of its four feet might shatter the spine of a hundred-pound wolf. Even a malnourished animal must be a formidable foe.

I had already noted the respect with which our hosts spoke

of the wolf, as if his presence were everywhere. Now I began to understand. Even when backed up by the pack, the wolf had a tremendous job before him in tackling a moose. No wonder the legends picture him as such a persevering villain!

We encountered two more moose along the way. Both were cows with yearlings at their sides. If these youngsters had been calves as young as six months old, we would have had to be careful, since a cow moose can be a dangerous foe who charges anything that moves as she protects her young calf.

After lunch we struck cross-country toward a spot marked X on Mike's map. It was a swampy area at the head of a tiny pond. Fanning out in a line, we slowly worked our way abreast of each other. We had gone about a hundred yards when my eye came to rest on a gray mass which covered the ground. It made a circle perhaps ten feet in diameter.

Mike Kochert saw it at the same instant. "Got it!" he yelled.

We had found what we were looking for. The gray circle turned out to be a mat of moose hair. It was a few feet away from the remainder of the animal: a skeleton and a few bits of hide. Here was where the moose had finally met the ever-present wolves.

Mike Wolfe bent for an examination. The antlerless skull told him it was a female. A male would still have had antlers, or at least bony bumps where they had been growing before they were shed.

Now came the vital part of the study. Why had this particular female been singled out to be killed? Was she old, crippled, malnourished—or had she just been caught at a disadvantage?

They found their answer almost at once. Mike Wolfe looked at the animal's teeth for a moment, then moved aside so the rest of us could see. It was apparent even to my un-

Russ W Buzzell

practiced eye that the teeth of this cow were worn down almost to the bone. More than that, though: somehow a mass of fibers and bits of twig had worked its way between two of the molars on the lower left jaw, creating a solid lump of tight-packed material about the size of a pencil. Spreading outward from this point the bone was black, soft and eroded in an abscess half the size of a golf ball.

Larry winced. "That must have been some toothache!"

And indeed it must have been. It was so bad that it may have prevented her from using the left half of her jaw at all. "So she had to do a lot of her chewing with the other side of her mouth," Mike Kochert said aloud as he jotted in his notebook, "and with no teeth to do it with, she must have been in a fine pickle. Winter's bad enough when you're healthy."

The autopsy continued. Working on such a sizable animal took something more than a scalpel and forceps, so part of their standard equipment was a hacksaw and a little hatchet. With these they trimmed away, learning what they could from the condition of the bones. One of the last spots to give up its nourishment for the use of the body is the bone marrow, since the fatty material is withheld for dire emergency. But in this case the emergency had arrived. Had we been able to examine the marrow cavity before decomposition set in, we would have found it empty, because the cavity was dry, not greasy.

After they had packed certain portions of bone for further study, Mike Wolfe hoisted his part of the load to his shoulders. Then he turned and faced me.

"Ron," he said, "you've seen it once. I've seen it dozens of times. And all the biologists who have been studying the wolves and the moose have seen it again and again. There have been more than four hundred dead moose examined in eleven years, right here on this island. At least half were killed by wolves. And over and over you could say the same thing: The wolves did the moose a favor. I wish you'd put that in your book."

He stopped for a moment, perhaps a bit surprised at his own intensity. Then he went on. "Some say that hunters should be allowed in here to cut the moose herd down to size," he continued. "Of course that's against National Park regulations. And think what it'd do to the wilderness character of the island! Right now the forest is more or less at peace with man: a single day of hunting would change all that."

Besides, he reminded us, the fatal moose build-up and crash had all occurred prior to 1940, before Isle Royale had become a National Park. So obviously the hunters had not done the job even when they were legal. On the other hand, since the advent of the timber wolves the moose population had roughly stabilized at perhaps nine hundred individuals. This is about one fifth of what there were in those black days of the mid-Thirties. Not that things are perfect now, in view of the fact that the moose still severely tax their food supply, especially in winter. But they have worked out a sort of dynamic balance with the wolf.

And, from the standpoint of the wolves, there is another angle. Often the claim is made that if predators are not checked, they will overrun the land. Yet these wolves have not exploded in numbers, even though they have had two decades to do so. They have remained at about two dozen individuals—one large pack and two smaller ones.

We had found our moose so early in the day that on the way back we took a side trip to where the wolves had killed another moose. Here the story was even more plain. It was a cow moose like the first, but, though her teeth were in fair shape, her bones were swollen with arthritis. Several of her joints were rough and gnarled, with thorny projections of bone. It was a look at her left hip, however, which led me to bless those wolves: it had practically no socket at all. Probably she had hobbled along on three feet, unable to run properly or to strike out at her enemies when caught.

It would take a mighty confirmed "varmint hunter" to blame the wolves, we decided after reading the story in those old bones.

Of course with our friends to interpret the signs for us, the tale was clear. Otherwise it would just have looked as if the wolves had killed a moose. Period. "Occasionally a camper finds the remains of a calf that's been killed," Mike Wolfe commented, "and if he dopes out what happened—or somebody tells him, he thunders to the Park Service that it must get rid of all the wolves. But sure, wolves take calves— every chance they get. After all, they're opportunists. So is every wild animal. What else would you expect?"

When they had taken all the samples they needed from this second moose we turned and started on the long trail back to Mike's cabin. And finally, back at our campground, Steve and I tried to patch together the details of that eventful day. We added up the score: eight live moose and two dead ones. Plenty of evidence of the great animals, too—tracks, bits of hair caught on stubs; branches broken and stripped of their twigs and foliage.

We'd also seen signs of the wolves. Their tracks, which could have passed for those of a large domestic dog, were common along the trail. Every little while we would come across a small heap of scats, or droppings. And since wolves are the dog's distant cousins, we weren't surprised when we discovered one particular stump they'd honored with their frequent visits—just as Rebel takes his daily turn at the base of our RFD mailbox back home in Vermont.

The more we talked with our friends in the next couple of days the more we were impressed with the special way in which they spoke of the wolf. They mentioned his name with obvious respect. To them he was the capstone of a living pyramid on the island. His presence was like the umbrella of a benevolent despot under whose shelter life could proceed confidently, surely.

I doubt that these Isle Royale naturalists scarcely ever consider the common ways in which we use the term "wolf"— the heartless masher who seduces innocent young women, for instance, or the fiendish money-lender who demands his pound of flesh. Furthermore, the "lone wolf," so popular in human fantasy, seldom exists in nature. Not in a normal situation, at least. Real-life wolves are social animals, with a strong sense of family ties. They have intense loyalty to each other and to the group. If one wolf is wounded, its mate may remain with it. If the wounded animal cannot travel at all, the mate will even bring food for it to eat.

Usually one animal—a dominant male—is the acknowledged head of the pack. He doesn't always lead the group on its hunts, but he takes for himself the choicest parts of food. When he visits from one member of the pack to another, he walks with a sure step, body erect, as befits a chief.

Below him, in a descending scale, come the lesser individuals in a regular "pecking order," with each wolf knowing its place in regard to others of its same sex. At the lower end of the order the boundaries are a bit hazy, with consequent shifting around. But even then a social climber must be able to prove his qualifications.

While fights are not uncommon, they are seldom fatal.

If a major issue is at stake—the leadership of the pack, say, or the attempt of an outsider to join the group—one of the animals may be killed. "Loners" have been observed trying to join a pack; although they seem pathetically eager to be accepted, the privilege is seldom granted. The unattached wolf lingers on the outskirts of the group and adopts every attitude of meekness, but one or more of the pack lunges after him if he gets too close. If he persists, he may finally be tolerated at a distance, but wolves that were too forward have been known to die from their wounds.

Occasionally a battle is joined in earnest. A wolf's jaws are perhaps the most powerful for their size among mammals; a single snap can break the neck of a deer. As one combatant closes in, his rival opposes him with the only invulnerable weapon: those fangs. For a while it is mouth against mouth. But both are seeking an opening, some moment of weakness that exposes a leg, a neck, a shoulder. Raging and slashing, they tear at each other. Finally one stumbles or slips —and the other is instantly on top.

Yet even in such dire straits there is still the chance for mercy. If one wolf is clearly getting the worst of it, there is still one final recourse it can choose: to surrender. The defeated wolf does this by ceasing to struggle and by turning its unprotected throat toward the attacker. The victor, almost as if bound by honor, refuses to deliver the final blow, since the vindictive lust to destroy totally other members of its own kind is a blot far more typical of man than of beasts.

The battle usually stops right there. A fight between females in captivity once went to this point. The winner placed those terrible jaws just above the throat of her opponent, with lips drawn back and teeth bared. Thus the two creatures remained for perhaps a full minute, neither making a move. Then, on some unseen signal, the tableau was ended. The victorious female turned and walked away. Carefully righting herself, the loser fled to a far corner of the large enclosure.

Such chivalry hardly fits the old notion of the insensate ravening beast. After all, wolves are scarcely doves. And, indeed, they are not: a dove may peck at another without mercy, pulling all the feathers out and biting at the naked skin until the vanquished is reduced to a bloody carcass. Chickens sometimes do the same, even going so far as to feast on portions of their dying victims. More than one aquarist has found a valued tropical fish reduced to a skeleton by the frenzied attack of another of its own species. But most people will tell you that the dove is an emblem of peace, the chicken is a coward, the fish lacks determination to do anything, and that the savage wolf is a savage wolf—even when he isn't.

Besides the position of defeat in battle, there are a number of other ways in which one animal demonstrates its attitude to another. When two wolves meet, they touch noses and sniff each other just as dogs may do. At first their demeanor is stiff and unmoving. Then the tails begin to wag—the tail of the lesser animal first. Or, if one animal is clearly dominant, the other may approach it with tail tucked between its legs and its ears lowered in submission, like a dog greeting its master. It may cringe and fawn like a puppy. In contrast, the dominant animal holds its tail high, like a banner.

Excited wolves may bark, just as their domestic relatives do. I have heard them bark in Alaska, and they sometimes bark on Isle Royale. While there is not a single authentic case of an unprovoked attack by wolves on man, they have occasionally been known to stand and bark at a person in the midst of some disputed trail. It was on the admittedly faint possibility of such a welcome that Steve Greene and I walked, ate and almost slept with our cameras right at hand.

We knew there was small hope of any photo, but we were more optimistic about the chance of hearing them howl. L. David Mech writes that the reason for the howling of the wolf is still unclear. Perhaps part of it is restlessness, somewhat as a human being may tap with a pencil or hum a tune. Perhaps it may serve to keep the pack together, or to announce that some activity is about to begin.

Whatever its purpose may be, the howl is one more demonstration of the sociability of the wolf. If one animal howls, others soon join. Biologists have recorded the howling of wolves and then played the tape back later; often this triggers a fresh response from the forest. Larry Roop pointed out that wolves may even respond to a long, drawn-out "hello-o-o"—though, luck being what it is, they didn't when he tried it for us this time.

Many an adolescent boy can give a creditable imitation of the cry of a wolf—or, at least, the coyote or brush-wolf, with its higher-pitched note. But to me, hearing the long, low, drawn-out howl in an Alaskan setting of utter solitude was to gain forever a treasured bit of the wilderness. Dr. Durward Allen of Purdue, mentioned earlier, wrote an article with David Mech in the February 1963 *National Geographic*. To them the chorus of the wolves was far from the horrible, blood-curdling, chilling cry of demons. Instead, in their listening ears it became "the grand opera of primitive nature."

Wolf pups are born in March or April "after the female has 'ordered' them like a lady dog in February," as one of my high school students delicately permitted herself to say in a term paper. The female has her litter in a rock cave or in a den which she has dug. Her half-dozen pups are blind and helpless.

The male is a model father. He has remained with his mate through the weeks prior to her confinement; now he accompanies the rest of the pack in a search for food. When he returns, he may trade places with the female so she can hunt. Or he may bring back a choice tidbit for her to chew on. He helps her bring the youngsters to maturity, often staying on with her for life.

Meanwhile the watery-blue eyes of the pups soon begin to change to the golden yellow of the adult. By the time summer has arrived, the youngsters begin to take an interest in the world outside the den. When one of the parents brings a bone, the pups attack it with all seriousness, growling and snarling in little puppy voices. In their play they tumble over each other, often including their dozing mother as part of their playing field. The great naturalist Adolph Murie tells about a litter of pups which played so hard all over five adults that the older wolves had to get up and move.

Wolves may even have babysitters. Not all the females bear pups each year, and sometimes a female with nothing else to do takes over the domestic duties. Then the mother jauntily bounces off to hunt.

While the youngsters are feeding on milk, the task of caring for them is simple. However, as they begin to require a meat diet, things become more complicated. To drag home a haunch of moose hefty enough to satisfy a household of active pups would be quite a job, and the pups aren't swift and strong enough yet to run with the rest of the family. What to do?

Nature, as always, has worked out the answer. Each parent crams down as much meat as it can hold—sometimes twenty pounds or more. This is quite a feat for a creature which, on Isle Royale, on the average weighs perhaps sixty pounds for females and eighty pounds for males. Then, trotting back to the den, the parents disgorge a good portion of the meal for the benefit of the pups. Partly digested and surrounded by food enzymes, the food is readily assimilated by little stomachs. The domestic dog that regurgitates its food and then swallows it again is behaving like some wolflike ancestor.

By autumn the timber wolf puppies are large enough to run with the parents. They begin to show the adult grizzled coat which gives them their name of "gray" wolf. They take their places beside their older brothers and sisters from the previous year. There may also be a spare aunt, uncle, or, to quote my fastidious high schooler again, "an extra mother wolf"—although there's small evidence of any eternal triangle. The result may add up to six or eight in a pack, depending on how many pups survive the summer.

In winter, two or three family units may band together for trailing and hunting. Dr. Mech found one large pack of about fifteen individuals on Isle Royale. Two small associations of two or three animals each brought the total to about twenty-two wolves, and the number remains quite constant over the years. Each pack has its own territory where it hunts and raises its young.

"From the air, when we watched the wolves hunting," Mike Wolfe told us, "it looked like an exercise in frustration. Not that they couldn't find plenty of moose. It was just that a moose that stood its ground was more than the wolves cared to tackle. They'd surround it and 'test' it for a few minutes, but if it wouldn't run they'd give it up as a bad job. One day we saw them test seven moose along the shores of Lake Richie. Not a one of the moose would run."

Recalling that our Vermont deer usually run from a dog, thus inviting pursuit, I asked him what difference it made if a moose ran or not. "Apparently if a moose tries to run, it's an admission of weakness," he said. "So the wolves chase it until they find what that weakness may be, hoping to catch it at a disadvantage. Even at that, they have to chase about a dozen for each one they do catch."

We decided that such an arrangement must keep both wolves and moose honed to a fine edge. But how did they react to the presence of an airplane over their heads?

"They don't even seem to notice us after we've been around awhile," Mike said. "Once, when we'd been absent for a year, they circled and jumped, almost like big, friendly dogs. But most of the time they pay little or no attention to an airplane in the sky. We just fly above them without chasing them."

I remembered a remark made by Douglas H. Pimlott in *The World of the Wolf*. The striking thing about the wolf—and the thing which had so impressed Mike that time—was the animal's friendliness. Not once did any of the dozens of first-hand reports about wolves, by those who really know them, describe wolves as rapacious, slinking monsters. Such beings harried Little Red Riding Hood and the Three Little Pigs, yes. The wolf at the door is this same kind of hideous creature, too. So is the villain in *Peter and the Wolf*. So is the fabled werewolf, who turns into a human being by day.

But on Isle Royale? Hardly. Nor on Mt. McKinley, where Adolph Murie slept right close to them. Nor in the only other two places where the wolf is protected by the National Park Service: Katmai and Glacier Bay national monuments in Alaska. Nor in the household of Lois Crisler, whose celebrated book, *Captive Wild*, shows these creatures for the loyal and affectionate animals they are.

In most other places, however, the wolf is to be destroyed on sight. Soviet Russia has committed itself to a policy of complete and final extermination of the European wolf, a blood relative of our North American animal. Belatedly, our national government has seen fit to place the wolf on the list of endangered species. In spite of this, in the state of Alaska— one of the few spots where the wolf could conceivably hold its rightful place as a part of the vanishing wilderness—in spite of this, every wolf killed in Alaska nets the proud hunter a bounty of fifty dollars. And to accomplish the deed as fast and comfortably as possible, the hunter may track the wolf down over the snowy tundra with a helicopter. He hovers over the animal at his leisure, firing away until his thrashing target is stilled.

For centuries man moved in on the wolf with his cattle and his sheep. When the wolf, understandably, helped himself to this bonanza, man went after him with fire in his eye. He decreed that the wolf must go.

The superb natural intelligence of the wolf, however, quickly taught him that man was to be feared: his guns, his dogs, his traps, his poison. The animals that survived the campaigns of slaughter, living by their wits, became legends: the white wolf of the Cheyenne, the Custer wolf, and King Lobo, whose fabled life was recounted by Ernest Thompson Seton.

I remember a visit to Wolf Den State Park near Putnam, Connecticut. Here a plaque is erected to the immense courage of General Israel Putnam, who pursued the area's sole surviving wolf to the rear of her den. There, according to one old account, "by the light of only a flickering torch, he shot the horrid creature to death."

Contrast this with Adolph Murie's story in his *A Naturalist in Alaska* of a visit to a wolf den:

> . . . I followed the tracks for a mile or more to a point where they climbed a bluff bordering the river bar, and there I surprised myself and a black wolf, a male. He ran off about a quarter of a mile into a ravine and howled and barked at intervals. Then, following tracks going out to the point of the bluff, I found the den. As I stood four or five yards from the entrance, the female furtively pushed her head out of the burrow, then, on seeing me, withdrew. But in a moment she came out with a rush and galloped part way down the slope, where she stopped a moment to bark. She loped away and joined the male, and both parents howled and barked from the nearby ravine until I left.
>
> I was sorry I had come upon the den in this sudden way, for I feared that the young would be moved and that I might fail to find the new location. From the den issued the soft whimpering of the pups. I could not make matters much worse, so I wriggled into the burrow, which was sixteen inches high and twenty-five inches wide, to investigate the young. Six feet from the entrance was a right-angle turn. Here the burrow was enlarged to form a bed which the female apparently had been using,

32

for it was well worn. But, with the melting of the recent snowfall, this bed was full of water, in which there was a sprinkling of porcupine droppings. A porcupine had used the den the preceding winter. The willows nearby had been barked by the porcupine in its winter feeding, just as the Tanana Indian had found the spruces barked near a den.

From the turn, the burrow slanted slightly upward from six feet to the chamber in which the pups were huddled squirming. With a hooked willow I managed to pull three of the six to me. Not wishing to subject them all to even a slight wetting in the puddle at the turn, and feeling guilty about disturbing the den so much, I withdrew with the three I had. Their eyes were still closed and they appeared to be about a week old. All three were females, dark, almost black. One seemed slightly lighter than the other two, and I placed her in my packsack to take back to camp and raise for closer observation and acquaintance. We later named this wolf pup "Wags," and she was to give us many interesting hours. Then I crawled into the den again with the other two and returned them to their snug chamber.

Although we spent several days on the island, Steve and I never saw a single wolf. We found their fresh tracks in the mud of a little stream a few hundred yards from our campsite, so we knew they were there—and, doubtless, well aware of our presence. But, for my part at least, I'd have to content myself with memories of the sound of barking at dusk and the drawn-out howl across an Alaskan valley years ago.

We had taken this trip in the expectation that the timber wolf would be an unseen wraith who remained beyond our sight and hearing. And such he proved to be, though his presence lingered over the entire island. Indeed, if we had seen a wolf, I would hardly have believed my eyes; it somehow would have been out of character for this great predator to allow himself to be surprised by mere human beings.

So we left Isle Royale, Michigan. Hugh Beattie, its superintendent, and Robert Rogers, the Chief Park Ranger, would soon find a new tourist season upon them. Radios would blare, barbecues flare. The wolves would retire to the wild areas between the trails. If the means were provided for them at that point, they would probably prefer to leave the island forever.

But summer would pass. The wolves would come back to the trails. They'd trot along the shore and investigate the campsites which had been so recently occupied. Then, gathering together, they'd sniff each other for a moment, tails wagging.

As they soundlessly trotted into the forest, the island would slip back into the past. For a few months this speck of land would once again become a part of that vast North American continent of old—before civilized man came to plunder the rightful inheritance of one of the noblest creatures on earth.

Rat

> **Rats!**
>   They fought the dogs and killed the cats,
>   And bit the babies in the cradles.
>   And ate the cheeses out of the vats,
>   And licked the soup from the cooks' own ladles,
>   Split open the kegs of salted sprats,
>   Made nests inside men's Sunday hats,
>   And even spoiled the women's chats
>   By drowning their speaking
>   With shrieking and squeaking
>   In fifty different sharps and flats.
>   **Robert Browning: _The Pied Piper of Hamelin_**

THERE are hundreds of books and articles telling what a fine creature the rat is. Really.

The trouble with these stories is that they are nearly all shelved in sterile laboratories or in the stacks of medical libraries. They languish, scarcely read by any but professional researchers, between the covers of magazines with ho-hum titles like *Animal Physiology*, the *Journal of Heredity* or *Biological Abstracts*.

Further, these accounts are so muffled in awkward, stilted language ("three of the test subjects evidenced fibrovascular recession, giving a neo-classic example of the Glommus Syndrome") that most such recitals have a short synopsis at the end of the article so you can tell what really happened. Nevertheless and despite any gobbledygook, those reports tell an amazing story.

They show how *Rattus norvegicus*—the common brown, or Norway, rat—has come to the service of mankind through the years. In these accounts he is wearing an immaculate white laboratory smock, but he is merely an albino variant of that creature that pokes through the rubbish at the dump or scuttles out of your way in an alley. Rattus the Scientist and Rattus the Scavenger are one and the same creature.

Much of what we've learned about heredity has been taught us by the rat. We understand our own behavior better after watching that of our pink-eyed, white-coated, four-footed teacher. Many a medical career has been launched after a squint at the fascinating innards of a white rat in a school biology lab. Cancer, arthritis, heart disease—to name just a few—are maladies whose comeuppance may depend largely on the laboratory rat. He has already done his stint in the wars on polio and tuberculosis, and has tried out such delights as zero gravity and high-G forces in the space program.

We owe him a great debt, which we can repay by demanding humane conditions for, and handling of, all living creatures used in scientific experiments, for much of our civilization rests on the narrow shoulders of this durable little rodent.

On the other hand, a great deal of our modern world is in danger of being toppled by the same creature. Here we meet our Dr. Jekyll when he is being the infamous Mr. Hyde. He's dressed in inconspicuous brown, thus blending in with almost any situation, especially under cover of darkness. Those same chisel-teeth that have taught us about minerals and vitamins are busy gnawing away at the very house we live in. If that house caves in, the rat will suffer too, for this one-pound nuisance is at his pesky best where human beings are at their worst: in crowded slums, dingy hovels and dirty waterfronts. A common rat abandoned in the woods or out in the meadow is out of its element. It quickly makes its way to the nearest habitation of man, its biggest friend and greatest enemy.

Fleas carried by rats were responsible for the grim toll of bubonic plague during the Dark Ages (we'll see how, in the next chapter). Murine typhus, the scourge of war, is spread by their lice. Estimates of damage to all kinds of material— food, textiles, lumber—vary tremendously, but the U.S. Fish and Wildlife Service says that every man, woman and child in the nation pays nearly two dollars a year in direct losses due to rats, whether they ever see a rat or not.

Yet you've got to hand it to him. In a world that has seen the tragic loss of the passenger pigeon, the great auk and the Carolina parakeet almost within the memory of people now living, the brown rat has flourished. In spite of traps and cats and poisons and campaigns, we still have rats aplenty. Again, estimates vary widely, but it's thought that there is at least one rat for each person alive in the world today. That's about five billion of the rodents. Eight thousand new rats—and people—are being produced every hour. Not bad, when you get down to it, for an animal that nobody wants.

How can the common rat do so well over the centuries? Why did it survive while the splendid Steller sea cow—a marine goliath twice the size of a walrus—was completely wiped out two decades after being discovered on a North Sea island? What kindly providence protected the rats on the ships of the sailors who sought the eggs and flesh of the last dodo?

The answer lies in the rat's ability to adjust to new situations. It can fit in almost anywhere. The Norway rat got its name from its occurrence on sailing vessels, with the busy maritime nation of Norway getting the credit. Actually the animal probably originated in Asia. It spread from one port to another as shipping flourished in the eighteenth century, apparently crossing the Atlantic about the time of the American Revolution. Here it tunneled its way through cellars and under wharves. The smaller black rat *(Rattus rattus)*—also an ocean voyager—took the other half of man's habitation, becoming the "roof rat" until gradually driven out by its more aggressive cousin.

Not only can rats go almost anywhere, but they can eat nearly anything they find when they get there. Almost any plant or animal food will do—plus some things that aren't food at all. Rats chew through heavy lead shielding on power cables. They chip away at old, crumbly concrete. They've been known to gnaw their way into a plastic swimming pool. And here's a possible source for the belief that elephants are afraid of mice: rats are fond of the fatty tissue of the toenails of the great pachyderms.

One of the reasons behind the rat's incessant urge to sample toothpaste tubes, Clorox bottles and shoe leather is the necessity to keep its teeth worn down. As with most of the rodents and the rabbits, the rat possesses a constantly growing set of incisors. If these teeth are not honed to size, the animal will starve. A rat that has lost an upper incisor, say, has nothing against which its corresponding lower tooth can wear itself away; in a few weeks the unopposed tooth will get so long that the rat cannot shut its mouth. If it manages to survive, its life will be terminated when the maverick tooth grows up in a semicircle and penetrates its brain. All told, a rat's incisors may grow more than six inches during his three years of life.

If you are in doubt about this creature's ability to adjust

to new conditions, try setting a trap. The intended victim seems to recognize it at once. Sometimes it even pushes the offending object around almost as if to make it snap. Then, after the trap has sprung, the victorious rodent consumes the bait.

A farmer I know even baits his traps with poisoned food; he figures he'll outfox the foxy rats. It works, too. "Why, I've been fooling the rats this way for years," he tells me. But the very fact that he gets a continuous supply of rats proves he never fools *all* of them.

Even professional ratcatchers, from the Pied Piper of Hamelin to the modern exterminator with his impressive apparatus, can seldom get every rat. A few are almost always left. If by chance the rodents are wiped out entirely, a few soon move in from next door. A well-fed female can produce in a year eight to ten litters of eight or ten youngsters each. Each of her offspring is ready to breed on its own in about four months, so the lucky householder is soon right back where he started.

Brother Rat makes his way right along with us wherever we go. He moved West with the pioneers. He went underground into the sewers and subways. There are rats living in the maze of railroad tracks beneath New York City who are born, raise their families and die without ever seeing the light of day.

These rodents have added much to our language. It's the rat that deserts the sinking ship; therefore he is a coward, though it would make no sense for him to remain. If you "rat" on somebody you betray him. Fight like a cornered rat, and you fight to the end—behavior that's fine in people but wrong in rats. Call a person a rat and you've said everything in that three-letter word, even if neither of you has ever known a single rat personally.

Whether we like it or not, the rat is a perfect adjunct to our activities. Sheltered from all harm, constantly supplied with garbage and packaged products free for the nibbling, kept warm in winter and cool in summer, he fares as well as many a pampered pet. Probably he gets along even better, for he can choose his own food.

The presence of the rat, reminding us of our own slovenly ways, is a constant source of embarrassment. He's one problem you cannot sweep under the rug. Since we've built him a refuge from hawks and owls, and since we take great pains to eliminate every skunk, fox and weasel before it can catch a single rat, we have only ourselves to blame. Like it or not, we've made the rat what he is today.

Our attempts to put our little fellow-traveler in his place have often taken the form of going after the symptoms rather than treating the cause. Instead of buckling down and cleaning up conditions that favor the rat, we've tried to get other creatures to carry out our campaigns for us. I remember once seeing a ferret released under a barn in Connecticut. There was a general alarm among the rats—squealing and chattering and the thumping of bodies frantically trying to escape. A few seconds after the ferret invaded their quarters, rats erupted from all over the barn and fled into the grass. But even the nimble ferret couldn't catch them all. Doubtless the remaining rats were back in a short time.

The rats in Hawaii got to be such a nuisance that the swift little mongoose was imported from Asia to deal with them. We saw the results when we visited the Islands recently: half a hundred species of ground-nesting birds exterminated completely, chickens and small wild animals in mortal danger of their lives, and mongooses all over the place.

The rats? Doing fine, thanks. It seems that the mongoose runs around largely by day, while the rat is abroad at night. So the paths of these two mammals seldom cross.

While rats make us uncomfortable by reminding us of our

own failings, other animals don't seem to be human enough to suit us. We are seldom content to let a dog be a dog, say, and bark and howl and do his doggy best at the fireplug. We take him out on a leash and studiously look the other way. We deodorize skunks and pull the claws out of cats. When I had a pet porcupine a few years ago, a well-meaning friend suggested I de-quill Piney—remove all thirty thousand of his stickers. And she was quite taken aback when she learned I'd had him a whole year and hadn't taught him a single trick.

People seem to have a compulsion to make animals into human beings. We train bears to ride bicycles and teach elephants to stand on their heads. We do not adjust to them; we make them adjust to us. Yet if adaptability is a measure of intelligence, who is the smart one?

It's in the field of learning-how that the rat comes into its own. Rats can be trained to run surprisingly complex mazes. They can learn to open boxes for the food that's inside. They can be taught to recognize a geometric figure or a letter of the alphabet on sight. These are just laboratory stunts, but they show that man's uninvited guest is gifted with a heaping supply of native intelligence.

It also has an outsized helping of just plain pluck. It takes a good cat to kill a full-grown rat. I once witnessed the spectacle of an enraged mother rat steadily backing up a Doberman pinscher. The dog had blundered into her nest while a building was being razed. The Doberman, apparently not wanting to submit to the indignity of an abject rout, retreated up a steep mound of debris. As he scrambled backward, he sent pebbles and sawdust rattling down into the face of the sputtering mother.

She backed him right up over the top of the cellar hole. While she performed the feat, a high-priced bulldozer operator, several sidewalk superintendents of unknown salary, and a sometimes-paid writer watched in complete absorption.

42

RAT

But lest you impugn the bravery of that Doberman, consider the experience of a friend of mine who cornered a rat in a garage. She jabbed at him with a rake—and he promptly climbed up the handle and chased her out into the driveway.

For such feats, plus the ability to carry out his own population explosion right in the face of everything man can throw at him, you can't help but admire Rattus. In a very real sense, he is what we have made him, every step of the way. Whether he's in his space suit, his lab coat or his bandit's cloak, you've got to hand it to him.

And hand it to him you'd better. Chances are he'll take it anyway.

Flea

> **The flea, though he kill none, he does all the harm he can.**
> **John Donne: _Devotions_**

"WOLVES I can understand," Don Brown admitted. "They're perfect for the book. I guess they're about the most misunderstood creature there is. And I can see why you're going to include things like bats and spiders. You can't help but feel a little sympathy when everybody's down on them. But where do you figure fleas come in?"

I pondered his question. I had been telling my old boyhood chum about the cast of characters in this book. Interested in his reaction, I jotted down his comments as each creature was discussed. But when I mentioned the flea he was incredulous. "That does it," he said. "I've been able to see something good

44

in the other creatures you've listed. But what saving grace can a flea possibly have?"

"Well, how about the reason you just gave, Don—that we like to cheer for the underdog? As long as people are so set against fleas, isn't it time somebody told them what fleas are all about? There are two sides to everything."

It was true. I once had a teacher who never gave true-false tests. She said there were few things in the outside world that were either completely right or totally wrong—so why try to make them so in the classroom?

This was the case for the flea, too. How could anybody judge for himself if his entire knowledge of fleas came from the few he'd seen hopping around on an itchy pup?

The flea is a distinct individual, for one thing. He probably has as much personality per pound—or per microgram, to bring things down to his level—as any creature going. He's had songs composed about him, poems written about him, fables and stories woven around his elfin little being. Not long ago I read a novel in which the mischievous heroine was nicknamed La Puce—the flea. Indeed, the impish Puck himself may trace his name back to the same irrepressible little sprite. So the flea comes well recommended—in story, at least.

Then there are his acrobatic powers. People are forever comparing the jumping ability of the flea with those of the horse or the kangaroo or human beings. And these powers are vital to a flea's welfare, too, in spite of what would seem to be a sheltered existence in the fur of some lucky dog. Add to this the offbeat life of the flea as a youngster, and you can begin to guess that it should at least have its day in court.

So herewith the story of *Pulex irritans*—which I think is a marvelous name for the human flea—and all his urchin clan.

The story could well begin with that most impressive of the flea's many talents: its fabled leaping powers. Apparently even the doughty flea outdid itself one day. A friend of mine took one look at a newspaper account of the miniature creature's latest antics and threw the paper down in disgust.

"Come on, now," he exploded. "Somebody's kidding. A flea that jumped nearly half a mile?"

I picked up the newspaper. My friend pointed to a column at the left of the page. "Not only that," he continued, "but it says here they had to catch it with an airplane."

I took the paper, expecting a joke. But it was true, every word of it. The facts were all there. It's just that the conditions were a little strange, even for a flèa.

It seems that man has long been curious about various layers of the atmosphere. He's sampled the air from balloons, rockets and airplanes. His samples have picked up errant mosquitoes, off-course flies and wayward bees—some from as high as six miles up. In their flight these insects may have run afoul of a rising thermal and been tossed into orbit, as it were. There have been less predictable astronauts, too: spiders, ants and caterpillars, for instance. And at two thousand feet the scientists picked up a flea.

It's easy to understand the spiders, ants and caterpillars. Crawling around in the open as they do, they could have been started on their protesting way by any little whirlwind. But a flea is different. If you have tried to extract one of these persistent critters from a long-suffering cat or dog, you know the flea won't leave unless it wishes to. And so, the newspaper concluded, that airplane's small passenger must have hopped off some animal and right out into a helpful updraft. End result: the longest leap on record.

This should scarcely surprise anybody who has ever met a flea. In spite of his wingless condition—complicated by utter blindness as a youngster, with little improvement in later life—the flea gets around almost as it pleases. In one way or another, it has made it from the tropics to the arctics, from the Old World to the New and back again. If a flea cannot hitch a ride on some warm traveling companion, it has been known to stow away in all sorts of places: packing crates, elevators, even fancy attaché cases.

In the process of carving out a living—literally, for its main weapons are a pair of tiny bladelike mandibles—the ubiquitous flea has developed some eleven hundred known species. Two hundred of these live in North America. Since the little creatures with the built-in pogo sticks aren't the easiest insects to catch and identify, the total number of species is doubtless far greater.

Although each flea generally prefers a certain animal, it may dine at several cafeterias when it has to. Nearly any warm-blooded animal or bird may come in for a little unwelcome attention on occasion. The fox that chases the rabbit may catch more than he bargained for. It's not hard to guess from its scientific name that the frustrating little speck known as *Cteno-cephalides canis* might occur on dogs, but it can thrive almost as well on cats. Likewise *Ctenocephalides felis*, the cat flea, may repay the visit. Some fleas just aren't fussy.

There are mouse fleas, rat fleas, even bird and bat fleas. Such improbable animals as mink and muskrat, spending half their lives in the water, take their own small crewmen down with them on every dive; the cushion of air trapped in the dense fur keeps the whole assemblage warm and dry. And one of the largest fleas on earth, nearly a quarter of an inch long, spends its adult career right where the action is—in the fur of the high-strung, ever-hungry shrew.

There's one flea you'll never find, however. Although you may have been singled out for its attacks, the creature known as the "sand flea" just doesn't exist—even if you catch a couple to prove it.

True, a whole host of biting creatures—from mites to tiny flies to low-level mosquitoes—have been saddled with the epithet of "sand flea." Then, too, certain fleas *may* get sidetracked in the sand, with disastrous results to your legs and ankles. But more about these later. Dodging the issue of the so-called sand flea slightly for a moment, we'll merely quote that farmer who saw the giraffe in the zoo: "I don't believe it," he said, as he turned away; "there just ain't no such animal."

No, sand fleas are entirely fictitious—bona fide ones, at least. Almost any flea you can name prefers to stay right with its chosen host instead of wasting its time in unproductive sand. Certain crustaceans and tiny primitive springtails occasionally are so named, it's true, but they're no more fleas than a crayfish is a fish. Then what *are* those critters that peppered you last summer?

To answer this question you must find out just how a flea gets the way it is. Just as with the chicken and the egg, it is always hard to know where to begin describing the life of an animal. But with fleas it's doubly hard. Any of the various stages may last only a week or nearly a year, depending on circumstances. Fleas are careless when it comes to timing; they can live as slow or as fast as conditions allow.

Probably we can start with the flea where we usually meet him—as one of Queenie's unbidden guests. Queenie, of course, never had fleas before; that ill-bred cur down the street is the critter that's responsible. If you happen to part the fur on your pet's back at the right moment, you'll see a brown, wingless, six-legged creature. In size and color it reminds you of those flat little sesame seeds on the top of a toasted dinner roll.

Just seeing a flea doesn't guarantee that you've got it dead to rights, though. You nab at it hastily—and find that you've caught a few strands of Queenie and little more. The flea has shouldered right out of your grasp. Or, if your luck is good and you capture the culprit between thumb and forefinger, you still have a ways to go. A mighty pinch—enough to spell instant destruction for any insect on earth, you think—and you relax your grip. As you open your fingers, away goes the flea in full stride as if he'd hardly been detained.

To decipher a flea's invulnerability, think of a watermelon seed. Its smooth, hard skin and flattened shape make it difficult to grasp. And the seed isn't even struggling to get away. Now reduce that seed to one-twentieth in size, and give it six frantically pushing legs to help it along. Then add the delightful refinement of a fiery bite that's been known to make a dog yip right out loud. Now, perhaps, you have an inkling of the battle that Queenie—and Bruin, and Reynard, and Lobo and Peter Rabbit, too—must wage on several fronts.

A single flea, scuttling out of sight into a forest of fur or feathers, merely looks like an animated piece of dirt. But wet your fingers so you can hold on to him, and then release him under water. While he struggles helplessly you can study him.

It takes a magnifying glass to see what really makes a flea a flea. As you squint at the little captive, you observe a creature that looks as if it had been caught in an elevator door. It's flattened so much that "it goes forward edgewise," as a small friend once informed me. It also sports a fringe of backward-pointing spines at the hind margin of each body segment. These spines—plus its narrow-gauge silhouette—help the insect force its way steadily forward through an animal's coat without slipping into reverse.

The spines also help it to escape from your grasp—or from the teeth of its irate host. In addition, they prop it against a convenient hair as it braces for a nip.

Many fleas have a collar of extra-heavy spines or a bristly "mustache" like Jeff in "Mutt and Jeff." Scientists meditate solemnly on the arrangement of all these bristles; they help in identification. Otherwise, when you see one flea you've seen them all.

The visible world of these mighty midgets probably consists of little more than light and shadow. Instead of the compound eyes of most insects, the adult flea has only one or two simple eyes on either side of the head; and some fleas don't have any eyes at all. Still, with food at your very feet and no horizon but a thicket of fur or feathers, what's there to see?

To inspect a flea's surgical kit, you'll need a microscope. The lancelike mandibles are thinner than a human hair, but they are incredibly sharp. After two pairs of palps have found the right spot to dig, those twin mandibles go to work like little jackhammers.

When they reach a blood vessel, the mandibles join with other mouth-parts to form two channels: a larger tube through which blood is drawn upward, and a smaller tube through which saliva is pumped into the wound. The saliva has two effects: (1) it keeps the blood from clotting and (2) it packs a wallop like an injection of white lightning. Galvanized into action, the outraged landlord serves a sudden eviction notice on his pesky tenant.

It is in such situations that the flea's astonishing legs come in. If you watch a flea moving through its native haunts, you'll note that it seems to progress by jerky motions, almost as if it was half hopping. This is more or less what is happening. The thighs of a flea's legs—especially the hind pair—are greatly enlarged for leaping. And if it's forced, it can really cover a surprising distance. Fleas have been known to hop twelve inches into the air and more than two feet horizontally. If a man could do as well in proportion, he could leap the length of two football fields or vault lightly to the roof of a forty-five-story building. (Actually such a comparison is not fair to the flea, because tiny muscles are proportionately much stronger than large ones; then too, there are things like gravity and wind resistance to consider.)

The skeleton of a flea is on the outside. Such external

armor is fine for a tiny insect, but it becomes an engineering
nightmare for anything much bigger than a beetle. Even most
crabs are pretty helpless when not buoyed up by the water
around them. The limit is reached with great crustaceans like
the giant crab whose legs are sold in neatly wrapped packages
in supermarkets: nearly the density of water, they move about
gracefully in their native element, but on land they are almost
helpless.

Aided and abetted by tiny size plus a benevolent law of
gravity—and kept honed to a fine edge by the constant attentions of its host—the flea finds life active but simple. It's largely
a matter of eat and run. Even at best, though, a flea seems to
live less than two years. There's always the chance that it will
suddenly be cut down in the prime of life, too. So the question
arises as to how it can bestow its inheritance.

Whereas in the mosquito family only the female feeds on
blood, both sexes of the flea can—and do—bite. As any dog
could tell you, a favorite spot for fleas is along the fur of the

back, but their excursions may take them from head to tail. Therefore it is usually only a matter of time before the sexes get together.

Nevertheless an animal's fur can get to be quite a jungle. Some fleas, faced with this obstacle to boy-meets-girl, apparently load the scales in their favor with a little serenade. They scrape their two hind legs against each other or against the abdomen. This produces a high-pitched squeak, inaudible to our ears: "I'm over here, just south of the shoulder blade."

The celebrated biologist Karl von Frisch, in cogitating on the voice of the flea, decided that if human beings were tuned in properly we could hear from the thick fur of a large dog a choral concert like that of crickets and grasshoppers in a grass field.

Mating may be only a brief alliance when the potential parents meet. Sometimes the tender moment lasts less than a minute. Then they head off in opposite directions, individualists that they are. But to insure that it all lasts long enough, the male is furnished with just the right set of claspers and hooks. These fit only the corresponding portions of a female of his own species. Thus, even though there may be more than one kind of flea in residence on a particular host, there's little chance of mistaken identity.

Since both partners may have to run for their lives at any moment, the female has a device to store the sperm until it's used. This refinement is in the form of a somewhat J-shaped organ, the spermatheca. Thus she may need only one mating to fertilize as many as five hundred eggs—her lifetime production, scattered over weeks or even months.

The egg of a flea is, relatively speaking, enormous, rather as if a hen had produced a grapefruit. White, oval and glistening, the egg is dropped with scarcely a pause by the female on her rounds. From there it rattles out through the fur or feathers and drops to the ground. Hence the unwilling host serves not only as a diner but also as a distributor. If he is heavily infested, he may sprinkle flea eggs wherever he goes. A friend of mine rescued a puppy which had been abandoned at a local dump. She gave it an old purple velvet cushion to sleep on. In less than a day the cushion looked as if somebody had salted it. Each "salt grain" was the egg of a flea.

Sifting down among the bedding where the animal lives, the egg comes to rest. If there is plenty of warmth and moisture, as from a litter of puppies which share the bedding, the egg may hatch in just a few days. If things aren't so hospitable it may take a month or more.

The new youngster is an un-flea-like as anything could be. Thin, white, segmented and totally without eyes or legs, it looks like a snip of white thread about one-sixteenth inch long. Like its illustrious parents, however, it is good at getting around. After it has cut its way out of the shell with a flinty egg-tooth, it begins to wriggle in search of food. Tiny spines on its body anchor it as it squirms forward, earthworm fashion.

Food is not long in coming. A baby flea, like a baby human being, samples almost anything it can put in its mouth. Its own eggshell serves as an appetizer. After that, all manner of plant and animal debris is acceptable fare.

One thing the youngster seldom eats, however, is fresh blood. With tiny, chewing mouth-parts it couldn't make a living this way if it wanted to. The only blood it gets is usually secondhand. It greedily feeds on the droppings of its parents when it finds them. In fact, many adult fleas continue to bite when they're full—thus, apparently, affording a continuous supply of predigested blood pellets to the blind larvae poking about far below them. The blood corpuscles are even crushed by miniature teeth in the crop of the parent. Thus parent and child get the maximum benefit from the same blood meal.

After a week or two of scrounging, the larva has increased its size severalfold. It molts a couple of times in the process, thriftily devouring the shed skin each time. Now, looking like an undersized, furry wisp of shredded cocoanut, it is ready to make its cocoon.

Spinning a flimsy shroud about itself, the flea enters the only quiet period it knows. The silk of its cocoon is sticky, like spider web, and soon attracts bits of dust and debris. These hide the occupant while it takes on the contours of adolescence.

Now those six efficient legs appear. So do the club-shaped antennae, plus the special receptacle on the head where they can be folded out of the way—a handy refinement that many a moose could use as he pushes through a dense forest. Those wicked stilettos take form, too, though their outlines are softened by the scabbards within which they are created.

Now begins a waiting game. Again, depending on the species of flea and the conditions around it, the pupa may last for weeks or months. If things are right, the flea may make its debut in twenty days. If things are not right, it bides its time.

And "things" may be more than just temperature and humidity. They may also include the jarring and jolting occasioned by the imminent presence of some large animal. Under such a circumstance, the flea hastily exits from its form-fitting armor. Drying hard enough to navigate in a few moments, it pushes out through its cradle. Then it launches itself in the general direction of its lucky new meal ticket.

At this point, enter the "sand flea."

Suppose you have put good old Spot out to board at a local kennel while you went on vacation. If you can bear the thought that Spot did indeed have fleas, he probably left numbers of his small compatriots in all stages of juvenile development when you took him away. As some fleas are commuters, hopping off on occasion to mate and lay eggs or just to change their outlook on life, Spot may have left a few adults as well.

Now, a couple of weeks later, there are dozens of fleas in the empty house. Normally you would have gotten rid of many of them in vacuuming or sweeping, but in this case they are all present—and all hungry.

Even though they belong to Spot, the fleas are not all that loyal. You come tramping into the house. The fleas hastily emerge from their cocoons and hiding places. They leapfrog onto your legs, and you've got "sand fleas." They couldn't possibly have come from your dog, you say: he's been gone two weeks.

It doesn't help, either, to plan longer vacations. Fleas have been starved for six months and come back scrappier than ever. It doesn't even help to oust your faithful dog in disgrace. Without him to trot about the rooms, collecting his rightful flock, the abandoned fleas have nobody to turn to but you.

Suppose, however, that you don't even have a dog, but you're still favored with "sand fleas." A lot of the bites you collect are occasioned by other small creatures, but "sand fleas" get all the credit. Then, too, a beach or picnic area is a favorite spot for mice, chipmunks and squirrels. When the life of one of these small gleaners is snuffed out, its fleas are suddenly abandoned. So, even though they hop on as you walk through the sand, they really don't belong there.

Granted that fleas exist—be they "sand fleas," rodent fleas (in case you're so blessed), or the fleas from somebody else's dog or cat—what do you do now? To quote a veterinarian friend, "It's no sin to have fleas; it's just a sin to keep 'em."

Fleas are not a new problem. Some of the old remedies still work. The meticulous European housewife who airs her blankets and bedding may think she's only freshening them in the sunshine. However, she's also making it difficult for human fleas to get started. Almost any flea likes nice, dark quiet places. When the American woman plumps the pillows in making the beds, she's hearkening back to an earlier day when all the bedding was shaken vigorously.

The old heavy carpet was a fine flea nursery. Now, with so many vinyl floors and with throw rugs made of inedible synthetics, even a baby flea has to scratch hard for a living. And just as soon as it finds a few cookie crumbs or a little dandruff where Rover snoozed, the whole works gets tossed into the washing machine. Add to this the howling blizzard of today's vacuum cleaners, and the creature's environment has gone from nursery to nightmare.

But still the flea persists. How can you put him in his place? Now that DDT, Chlordane and others of their ilk have been exposed in their true colors, how can one go after a flea with something besides a washing machine and a vacuum cleaner?

Our forefathers knew about such homely remedies as pyrethrum and rotenone. These plant derivatives still work. In powder form they can be sprinkled in an animal's bedding. As a low-concentrate dust they can be fluffed through your pet's fur. The dust will do little harm to the animal even if eaten; this is a boon to cat-lovers, whose pets constantly lick and groom themselves. You can buy pressurized sprays with pyrethrins just made for use on pets. Methoxychlor is another low-risk product.

A farmer's wife I once knew had a wooden box for her dog behind the kitchen stove. In the summer she picked a double handful of a certain little daisylike flower and placed it in the box. She dried more stalks of the flower for winter use. "My mother taught me this," she said. "It's something they used to do in the old country. It seems to keep the fleas away. Sometimes she braided the stems and flowers into a collar and put them around the dog's neck, too."

The flower, in case you hadn't guessed, was daisy fleabane. It is a common weed along our roads and fencerows in summer. Apparently it works, too, or at least my friend claimed it did on Lassie. After all, fleabane is a first cousin of the chrysanthemum, and pyrethrum comes from a chrysanthemum.

On the subject of flea collars, it's hard to believe that a gadget around the neck will kill a flea on a dog's tail. Actually it is effective because fleas are such wanderers, and sooner or later they come in contact with the insecticide. But there are collars and there are collars. Mitzi, a small four-legged canine friend of mine, got such a rash from her flea collar that she lost half the hair of her neck, scratched herself raw, and ended up seeing a veterinarian.

So, if in doubt, get expert advice. A few fleas are better than a poisoned pet. As David Harum observed, "A reasonable amount of fleas is good for a dog. They keep him from broodin' on bein' a dog."

So far we have communed largely with dog and cat fleas. But there are more than a thousand other named species. Many of them have the same life history—with "woodchuck" or "wild swine" in place of "dog" or "cat."

Perhaps the most famous flea is the human flea, in its role as the star of the old-time flea circus. To screen his potential actors, the owner would put some fleas in a squat covered container. Most of them would jump themselves silly, banging against the roof of their prison in an attempt to escape. A few, however, would soon give up the futile attempt; and upon this indication that they possessed a smidgin of intelligence they would be chosen for careers in show business. Fitted with a delicate harness, such a "trained flea" performed wondrous feats. It pulled tiny wagons and provided the motive power for diminutive merry-go-rounds. It engaged in Lilliputian chariot races and hauled miniature cannon into battle.

Like as not, the flea's master himself provided the grand finale. Picking up his charges one by one, he treated them to dinner right on his arm.

The human flea, sometimes called man's closest companion, lives in the seams of clothing or in a tangle of unkempt locks and beards. It seldom bothers clean-shaven, mini-skirted, bikini-clad, deodorant-scented, drip-dry humanity. With our unwashed brothers, however, it fares more easily. And in areas where a change of clothing is a real problem—in the arctic regions, for example—the flea is right in its element. (A friend of mine who exchanged parkas with an Alaskan trapper soon discovered that he had got more than the fur coat he'd bargained for.)

The sharp discomfort of the human flea's bite may be just the beginning. The creature can carry disease from one person to another: murine typhus, for instance, or even an occasional case of bubonic plague—the Black Death.

The actual culprits in the spread of the plague are the common rat and its small cohort, the rat flea. Many scientists think that the plague was originally a disease of rodents. The germ causing it is found almost world-wide in a number of these little mammals. But when Europe was overrun with rats in the Dark Ages the stage was set for a disastrous transfer to human beings.

Pasteurella pestis, the plague bacillus, swarms in the blood of infected rats. The rat flea, in feeding, imbibes some of this lethal cocktail. The bacteria multiply enormously in its microscopic innards, increasing so fast that they may utterly block the food passage.

Now the rat flea is caught in a dilemma: it is starving with its stomach full. At the same time its ailing host may have expired. Desperate for food, the flea hops from one animal to another—even to human beings—vainly trying to satisfy its hunger. In the process it voids some plague-laden excrement, and this the victim may scratch into the wound made when the flea bites. Or, alternately pumping and sucking, the flea mixes the bacteria with what little blood it can cram down its gullet. Then, still trying to feed, it injects part of the resulting concoction into the next victim.

Apparently this is what happened in fourteenth-century Europe. One after another, people fell prey to the Black Death. Nobody understood how it spread. Authorities burned the beds, the clothing, the homes of the victims. They even burned the sick persons themselves. Suspecting witchcraft, they tried to stamp the disease out by torture. Finally, when the plague had run its course, twenty-five million people had died. This represented one person in four over the entire continent. And, although we think of bubonic plague as a medieval disease, some half-million people still die of it in India each year.

The disease continues in some kinds of wild rodents as sylvatic plague. Fortunately it seems to maintain itself in a more or less benign form. But as long as rats and mice roam the gutters and alleys there's the potential danger that a virulent strain might develop. It was partially because of this danger and partially to control louse-borne typhus that DDT was developed and used so lavishly in World War II.

In case you wonder about the difference between the flea and the louse, the flea is compressed laterally as if caught in a sliding door, while the louse is flattened as if beneath a heavy weight. Lice cannot jump, but merely crawl among the hairs of animals and the feathers of birds. Many of them, like the notorious "crab" louse, have lobster-claw gadgets on their legs to help them cling to their unwilling hosts. Lice attach their eggs, or "nits," to the outer covering (hair, feathers, clothes) of the host, and thus may never leave home for many generations. Obviously the impertinent leaping flea with its double residence, as it were, has far more personality than any stodgy louse.

Although fleas are much the same, there are variations on the theme of six legs, no wings and—well, a flea-shaped body. There's the delightful chigoe or burrowing flea of the tropics, for instance. This is different, by the way, from the "chigger" of southern grasslands, a tiny red mite more closely related to the spiders.

Normally the chigoe helps itself to any warm-blooded meal it can find, with a preference for people. The males and virgin females behave this way, at least. But when a female is expecting a few hundred eggs, she drops to the ground, where she matures for a while. Then she burrows into the skin or beneath the toenail of a passer-by, leaving just her tail section exposed.

Swelling to the size of a small pea, she creates a severe infection and pain. In some tropic lands it is common to see people with one or more toes missing because of the unwelcome aftermath of the visit of a chigoe. Meantime, the female drops her eggs occasionally, "seeding" the ground beneath her wherever her victim walks.

Poultry-raisers smear on lard or sulphur ointment for the sticktight flea, which finds a spot of exposed skin—usually around the eyes and comb—and stays there in such numbers that it may blind its victim. Dens of hibernating woodchucks, attracting rabbits, skunks and rodents, may become so infested that by spring everybody is sharing in everybody else's good fortune.

Even if the flea escapes all the nips and scratches and blows aimed in its direction, it may not get off scot free. The rat flea has its own tribulations, as we've seen, for plague may be just as fatal to fleas as it is to people. Rabbits in Europe and Australia, suffering from myxomatosis—which may well have been carried by their fleas in the first place—finally die, leaving their star boarders with the question of where to go next.

Other fleas have their problems, too. I remember stopping by the road to investigate a gray squirrel which had been killed by a car. As I reached down and stroked it there was a general stirring in its fur, almost as if the rodent were flexing its muscles. The squirrel's inhabitants, which had been clinging to the only home they knew, were running gratefully toward this new source of warmth and companionship. As they were squirrel fleas they wouldn't have found solace for long on my alien person, anyway. But this wasn't going to deter them from trying.

From the viewpoint of the flea, dipping into the bloodstream of its host is perfectly normal—only an extra straw in the soda, one might say. Yet the unwanted guest meets resistance at almost every turn. And one of the unkindest cuts of all happens while the common dog flea is still a baby.

Poking through the debris of the dog's bed, the larva is just minding its own business. But, as sometimes happens, its four-legged friend has a tapeworm. The eggs and segments of this unseen interloper are passed out in the dog's excreta. A few eggs get into the bedding. Along comes the flea larva on its buffet lunch. It mows its way right up to a tapeworm egg, swallows it, and keeps on going.

Then begins what must be, for the flea larva, a whopping case of indigestion. The egg develops into a little bladder-shaped object called a cysticercoid. Now the flea has a parasite of its own. Hindered by the presence of its unbidden guest, the flea may be just a bit too slow when the dog takes a nip. The dog, biting and licking, gobbles up the flea. And the tapeworm? The cysticercoid breaks out of its unfortunate incubator—and a new tapeworm is on the way.

These are just a few hazards of a life of ease. But fleas have apparently been able to withstand everything fate has thrown their way for a long time. The earliest known flea apparently hopped off some disgruntled mammal and right into a glob of sticky tree resin. Now, forty million years later, the flea is perfectly preserved in that resin, which has hardened into Baltic amber.

Nobody knows what distant relatives have fallen by the wayside as the flea skipped into the twentieth century, because it's difficult to decide from what roots the jaunty creature may have sprung. Some biologists link it to the flies. Others say it is closer to the sucking bugs and aphids. Scientifically the flea is placed in its own Order, Siphonaptera—literally, "the tube without wings"—which doesn't help at all in looking up its genealogy.

Of course, the little nonconformist is fully aware of where it fits best, even though it doesn't actually think things out that far. The flea in its furry forest is as much at home as the clam in its mud flat, the rabbit in its briar patch or the eagle in its aerie.

This gives me one more answer to the question my friend Don Brown posed in the beginning. What does the flea have to recommend it, indeed? Just the very fact that, in these times when everybody is trying to find himself, the flea is so perfectly and comfortably at home.

Even if a few million uncomfortable hosts don't happen to agree.

Mosquito

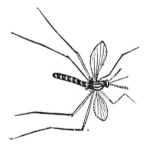

> The peopled region is peopled chiefly with monsters and moschitoes.　　　　　Walter Savage Landor: *Pentameron*, 1853

ONE of the major surprises that came as I learned about wild creatures was that there actually is something good about a mosquito. Strange as it seems, those buzzing hordes that drive you out of your lawn chair and those solo performers who rob you of a night's sleep *do* have their redeeming features. As with all living creatures, they have a place in this world. It really isn't necessary that every plant and animal fit in with our scheme to be of value on earth. After all, a weary planet might well ask of Man, if it could, "What good are *you?*"

In the case of mosquitoes, some of them are vital to the normal life of a pond or stream. They are a link in the food chain from algae to minnows to game fish. Many serve as bacteria traps in stagnant water. Some are even downright beneficial, catching and killing other mosquitoes.

It's usually hard to judge the group from the individual. Mosquitoes can be just as individualistic as people. The one I saw last summer was a good example.

I discovered this little lady in a most unusual place. She wasn't where she was supposed to be at all: on a bit of moss in a swamp, or poised hopefully on the potato chips at a beach party. She was in one of the swankiest office buildings in New York City—square above my head on the wall of the elevator.

I punched the button. The door closed, and we rode up to the twentieth floor together, that little mosquito and I. All the way, the ceiling loudspeaker played its music—apparently just for the two of us. When I got out, someone else called for the elevator. The door closed softly and the obedient elevator continued on its way with its tiny passenger.

What had caused her to wander so far from her native haunts? One expects mosquitoes at picnics, yes. And one includes them on fishing trips. But here on the twentieth floor in Rockefeller Center?

The mystery perplexed me. I couldn't forget that fragment of life up there on the wall, serenaded by the ghostly orchestra in the ceiling. Intrigued, I looked at the lives of these familiar little creatures with new interest. And almost at once I realized one thing: they are not as familiar as I had thought.

That automated little lady, for instance, might not have been so very far from home at all. In spite of the scarcity of swamps on Broadway, there were still plenty of places to give her a start in life. Although all mosquitoes need water for their babyhood, the water doesn't have to be out in a stagnant pond somewhere. Almost any spot will do for these durable opportunists—a tin can open to the weather, a clogged rainspout, the hidden pools in a street drain. Blessed with very little spirit of reverence, mosquitoes will blithely appropriate the flower urns in a cemetery, too. They've even been found in holy water fonts.

Having been hatched in some such place, perhaps, my mosquito had spent a hasty childhood in her prefabricated nursery. Now, as a full-fledged adult, she had risen above her original surroundings. With luck, she might dine on somebody during his coffee break. Then, with more luck, she'd make her way back to the open world.

This was just one of many feats performed by the impudent critters. In the process of complicating life for an arctic bear, an African baboon or an American bikini bunny, they have come up with fascinating diversification. For instance, to balance the deadly malaria mosquito, there are kinds that couldn't bite you if they tried. Others flit like a bee from flower to flower. One tropical species accosts ants like a tollkeeper, somehow persuading them to regurgitate a drop of liquid, which it swallows. And don't forget those mosquitoes which kill and eat other mosquitoes.

To understand these talented insects better, we might follow them through a typical life story—although, with some fifteen hundred species in the family Culicidae (which, sensibly enough, can be translated "the mosquito-like ones"), it is hard to pick out any one life story and call it typical. Better, perhaps, to say that they all play their own variations on a single theme.

Even in egg-laying there are different ways of doing things. The looks of my undersized urbanite tagged her technically as "the domestic mosquito"—a term given to her by straight-faced scientists. (At least I assume they're straight-faced, although "domestic" speaks to me of canaries, dogs and other pets.) She would probably seek out a bottle or old tire casing similar to the one where she had been raised. Her eggs would have been stuck together in a little raft, there to float on their pint-sized ocean.

If she had been any of the hundreds of other types, she would have parceled her eggs out a little differently. She might have scattered them singly over a marsh, perhaps, as the malaria mosquito does. If she'd been one of the yellow-fever mosquitoes, she might have laid them on the dry earth of some low spot; there the eggs might wait a year before they got flooded enough to hatch. According to her species, she might have bestowed her blessings on the water in a hollow log, the puddle of a concave rock or even the little pool in the vaselike leaves of a pitcher plant.

It doesn't take those eggs long to develop into "wigglers," or larvae, once they are wet. Mosquito nurseries are often here today and gone tomorrow, and life must be lived in double time. The eggs of the notorious salt-marsh mosquito, for instance, are faced with playful tides which may leave them stranded in the morning and wash them out to sea in the afternoon, so they may hatch out a day or two after they're laid. Other mosquitoes go them even better, sometimes hatching in a morning.

One of our commonest types, sporting the name *Aedes vexans*—an epithet given it, no doubt, by some frustrated scientist—helpfully supplies plenty of uninvited guests for your barbecue. This it does by the simple process of having only a few of its eggs hatch at any one time. There are always plenty of spares handy. Thus, just as you think a dry spell has gotten rid of them at last, a good rain brings on a whole new crop.

The wiggler is the most vulnerable stage of the mosquito. Shaped like a legless caterpillar with an outsized head on one end and a hollow breathing tube on the other, it somersaults

66

its way through the water. Opening and closing its body like an overactive jackknife, it makes a lively morsel for minnows and other fish. When I was raising tropical fish I used to keep an old pail of water out on the back porch. Its periodic wiggler population was a good supply of live food for my finny charges.

Those wigglers are regular little aquatic vacuum cleaners. Fringes of bristles, known as oral brushes, surround the mouth of a wiggler. When it is hungry—which is most of the time, for mosquito larvae may eat double their weight in a single day—it sets the brushes in motion. These create a tiny whirlpool, sucking bacteria, algae, yeasts and tiny aquatic animals into the vortex. A single hungry wiggler may "filter" as much as a quart of water per day.

A few mosquito larvae have improved on this general scheme. Their oral attachments include stiff projections, like ice tongs, with which they seize their unsuspecting cousins. In spite of the fairly good eyesight enjoyed by mosquito larvae in general, the victims never realize their danger until it is too late. If several of these predatory larvae get in a little puddle, they do away with every available larva. Then, still hungry, they start in on each other until there's only one left.

Although mosquito wigglers are a common sight, it is amazing just how common they really are. They multiply with an exuberance that makes you wonder why mosquitoes don't carry you away bodily. One inquisitive scientist took a census of the thickened gunk in the bottom of a shrinking puddle. His result: more than a thousand wigglers to a pint of water.

Naturally there must be some leveler, or the mosquitoes would inherit the earth—which many a disgruntled vacationist thinks they're about to do anyway. Water tigers and other predatory insects take their toll. So do salamanders. So do ducks and geese, guzzling in the shallows at the edge of a pond. Then, too, a good sunny morning could dry up that pint of water, thus giving those thousand mosquitoes their comeuppance in one fell swat.

Man tries to hasten their demise in a number of ways. Most mosquito larvae spend much of their week or ten days near the surface of the water, poking those rear-mounted breathing tubes up for air. One time-honored way to discourage such activity is to spread a film of oil on the water; the oil apparently clogs their snorkels. This fails to work well with a vicious biter known as Mansonia, however. It attaches its air hose to underwater plants and breathes oxygen from the pithy stems.

Then, too, thousands of acres of swamps have been drained and filled in the name of mosquito control—although admittedly this has been hard on the fish and ducks and water tigers and salamanders. It helps little, of course, to remind ourselves that the mosquitoes—and the ducks and fish—were here first. The prospect of all that new real estate where a marsh used to be is a pretty strong selling point. Besides, we can always put up a zoo, or at least a city park, with its garden pool, suitably treated with pesticides for mosquitoes.

If the wiggler doesn't get its fill of poison or oil, and if it doesn't end up as a tidbit for some passing predator, it undergoes a remarkable change at the end of a week or ten days. Just as a caterpillar turns into a cocoon, the mosquito larva becomes a pupa. Unlike most insect pupae, however, it is surprisingly active. Looking like a tadpole with a jointed tail, the swimming mosquito is now known as a tumbler. Although it doesn't feed in this stage, it still breathes—now through twin tubes poking up from what might correspond to the shoulder region.

The tumbler's life at this point is like that of an animated yo-yo: up to the surface for air, down at the slightest hint of

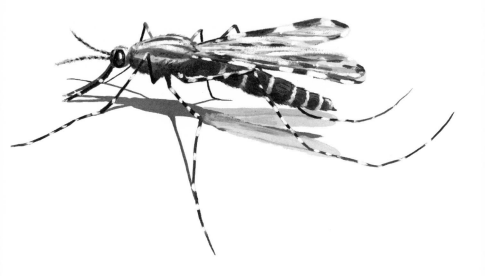

danger. Since its pupal skin is transparent, it can see the approach of enemies.

The tumbler stage may last only two or three days before the final transformation to adult takes place. But in this quick review of the remarkable changes in the mosquito's life, you've got to give the creature a good helping of admiration. As a wiggler it resembles little more than a hyperactive worm. It has no legs, no wings—just a body and a head with those swirling little mouth brushes. It breathes through a tube, plus a few gills which absorb a bit of oxygen from the water. Then in two or three short days it must turn into an entirely new creature. When it matures it will have six legs and a body defined in three distinct parts. It will also have functional sex organs, feathery antennae, a breathing system arranged like portholes along the body, wings with an exquisite tracery of veins—and, of course, that impertinent beak.

It is really phenomenal, this change from larva to adult. It is like turning a jeep into a jet in a couple of days—all the time driving the jeep at sixty miles an hour.

When the change is finally completed, the mosquito is ready to become airborne. This is a good trick in itself, for the tumbler has no way to climb out on dry land. But the resourceful mosquito has the problem licked. Rising to the surface, it lies there a moment with its back awash. A split appears in the outer skin along the midline. Straining and pushing, the soft mosquito forces the split to widen. Pumping air into its body through those brand-new spiracles along its sides, it slowly expands as it works its way up and out of the floating pupal case.

The mosquito's wings, antennae, beak and legs have been laid back closely along its body. Now it carefully frees them, one at a time, clinging precariously to its hollow shell. It pumps air into the veins of its wings by rhythmic motions. Finally, like inflatable toys, the wings expand into shape.

Occasionally I have come across these callow new individuals. They're light in color, almost transparent. Loath to strain those new wings, they spend the first twenty-four hours resting. Finally, body hardened and marked with the bands or splotches which identify their particular species, they launch themselves out on an unsuspecting world.

Nor are their intentions always as wicked as we make them out to be. It is just that they're great opportunists. Many of them apparently exist for the sole purpose of helping themselves to your blood, it is true. Many others, however, aren't so fussy. If no blood is available, they'll subsist on nectar, fruit juices or the sap oozing from a broken twig.

The males are far better behaved than their mates along this line. Simply stated, they are biteless. I've had males land on my skin and poke around hopefully, but their mouth-parts just aren't equipped to do the job. Like it or not, a male mosquito must remain a vegetarian.

By the way, it is easy to tell a male from a female. Both sexes have a slender proboscis sticking out in front, but the

70

male also sports a pair of conspicuous plumed gadgets called palps. Then, he also has large, feathery antennae compared to the skimpy feelers of the female. These last appendages apparently vibrate when stimulated by the high-pitched whine of the female's wings. Thus turned on, the male can use his antennae as a sounding device to help him "home in" on his lady.

Actually the lethal-looking beak of the female is not what does the job, either. The beak is merely a split sheath, like a scabbard, for the working tools: six hidden stilettos.

Knife-pointed, toothed, finer than a hair, these tiny lancets slice their way rapidly through the skin. The enclosing sheath strengthens them, doubling back as they enter. They probe around beneath the skin like a questing finger until they find a capillary or other tiny blood vessel. Sometimes the lancets assume a right-angle bend as they enter the vessel itself.

Once she is on target, the female forces an anticlotting saliva into the wound. When you feel the itch, it's largely the effects of this saliva. At the same time a pharyngeal pump begins a pulsating suction—and you've got a mosquito bite.

Adventuresome as she seems, that little lady often must have things just right before she will take even a wee nip. This may seem contrary to the way the mosquitoes never seem to stop, but chances are they are merely taking turns. Some species will bite only in the shade. Others wait until dusk. Still others will transfer their attentions from you to your dog, or vice versa—whichever is handiest.

The yellow-fever mosquito of southern climates often has a different way of compounding your misery. Landing on a shoe top or shirt collar, she walks until she comes to thin clothing or bare skin; thus you do not feel her alight. Then, when she bites and you go to slap her, the clothing moves and gives her a warning. Luckily, yellow fever has been almost eliminated in this hemisphere.

Assuming there exists such a thing as a typical mosquito, this is how she might like to have her meal prepared:

She'd rather bite through dark clothing than white. She seems to prefer muggy weather to good; darkness to sunshine; heated skin to cool; and calm air to a breeze. She's also attracted by the carbon dioxide and moisture in your breath.

So, if you'd be free of mosquitoes do these things: Take a cold shower and put on some light-colored clothing. Go outside only when it's clear, sunny and windy. And don't exhale.

Mosquitoes so bedeviled the Lewis and Clark Expedition, Captain Meriwether Lewis recorded in his Journal, and were so numerous that the explorers frequently got them in their throats as they breathed. But if mosquitoes are bad for human beings, they're sometimes far worse for wild animals. A naked baby bird may be drained of its blood by hordes of them. Snakes, frogs, turtles and mice come in for their share of attention, too. Even a basking fish, lolling in the shadows with its back just out of water, may be bitten.

Fawns may be so weakened that they are unable to nurse or to follow the female. Often a deer will go into a lake to escape the mosquitoes, submerging itself to the nostrils. If there's no deep water around, the deer may lie down in a stream. Its body acts as a dam, creating a little pond. The cool water finally rises to the top of the "dam," running over in a soothing flow.

The greatest misery for us, however, is not caused by the bite, but by the aftermath. Mosquitoes can carry dengue, or "breakbone fever," encephalitis, elephantiasis—and malaria. It has been estimated that one out of every two infectious disease deaths is caused, directly or indirectly, by malaria. If the chills and fever don't get the victim they weaken him terribly. Then he is a pushover for the next sickness that comes along.

For what consolation the fact provides, though, the mosquito may suffer as much from malaria as her victim does.

72

MOSQUITO

The carrier of the disease, a *femme fatale* known as Anopheles, can be told from other mosquitoes by her habit of resting her straight, slender body at an acute angle to any surface, as if poised like a dart. When Anopheles takes in a blood meal containing the malarial parasite, the microscopic invader penetrates the insect's stomach. There it multiplies, forming cysts on the stomach wall. Sometimes it even kills its host.

If the mosquito survives, the cysts break and release hundreds of new parasites. Some of them make their way to the salivary glands. There they lie in wait, ready to be injected into a new victim when the mosquito gets her next meal.

Apparently a blood meal is essential to egg development for many mosquitoes. Perhaps this is one reason why they are such vicious biters: it's either do or die, as far as any future generations are concerned.

There are many other oddities to their reproductive life. The sexual apparatus of the males, for instance, is an astonishing assortment of gadgetry. It is so distinctive that almost any species can be told by what scientists designate as the terminalia. This consists of hooks, plates, spines and claspers, and will fit only the corresponding arrangement of the proper female. To make it more intriguing, some mating may take place in mid-air, ceasing the moment the preoccupied couple hits the ground. Hence all that complex equipment may see service but briefly.

There are also all kinds of mating behavior. The males of some species gather in a gigantic swarm, dancing up and down over an object on the ground. Sometimes this is just a hummock or a boulder; sometimes it is a treetop. And sometimes it may be a person. If the person tries to walk away, the embarrassing swarm goes along, too. I recall a squadron review in the Air Force: the colonel who inspected us went solemnly up and down the ranks, unaware of the mosquitoes cavorting in the air over his head.

After the males have danced for a while in this exuberant stag line, they are joined by the females. Each female flies into the swarm, mates with the swain of her choice, and flies away to begin a new crop of wigglers. The high-pitched hum of the matchmaking may be heard half a hundred feet away.

In one variation, the couples remain together for a longer period. Dropping out of the crowd, they retire to a grass blade for a brief honeymoon. Sometimes they dance up and down in front of each other as a preliminary. Other times they merely remain attached in what might pass for togetherness until they go their individual ways.

Another technique for finding mates reminds you of the boys at the local drugstore. The males hang around some large, attractive animal—a cow, perhaps, or a man in a hammock. Then when a female comes along some lucky Lothario will win her.

The most startling behavior, perhaps, is that of a mosquito of New Zealand. As soon as the male can travel after leaving the pupa, he skates watchfully over the surface of the pool. Alert for every little motion, he even thrusts his head beneath the water. At last he finds what he's looking for: a female tumbler about to emerge. As she splits her skin he helpfully forces his way in beside her and mates with her before she has fully left the pupal shell. Often both of them are on their way to parenthood before either can fly.

These are just a few of the examples of how it is to be one of these undersized flies. And flies they are, speaking scientifically. In fact, the word "mosquito" is Spanish for "little fly." They bear the unmistakable mark of the Order of the Fly, too: two wings, instead of the customary four borne by most insects. The second pair has been reduced to two knobby

74

structures known as halteres, which vibrate in apparent frustration when the wings are in motion. But the halteres are more important than they look; cut one off and the mosquito spins, stalls or even flies upside down.

The mosquito's preoccupation with finding a blood meal has been pressed into service by a larger relative. One of the bot flies—a creature which burrows beneath the skin of an animal and develops there as a grub—buzzes around until she finds a mosquito. Capturing it, she lays her eggs on the struggling creature. These eggs hatch into tiny grubs. They cling to their unwilling babysitter until she alights on some warm-blooded animal. Then they drop off in response to the body heat and burrow into the skin of their new host.

Even if a mosquito escapes the unwelcome attentions of a bot fly or manages to dart away just ahead of a well-aimed swat, its adult life is likely to be on a short fuse. Those dragonflies which cruise over the ponds and meadows are wonderful mosquito traps. So are the warblers and swallows by day, plus the bats by night. And, barring every hazard imaginable, the road is still short. In the North, the lives of most males are snuffed out with the first hard frost. A few of the females may sleep until egg-laying season next spring. Many, however, die after they pass the torch to overwintering eggs or wigglers. Even in the South with everything going for it, a mosquito may hum its last within two to four months after it was hatched.

So there they are, those perky little optimists. Scientists say that they have withstood everything life has aimed at them for forty million years—perhaps longer. Thus they may have been around to bid farewell to the last dinosaur. They probably gave the first cave man a suitable welcome, too, some million-plus years ago. And since some determined mosquitoes—those Jersey bogtrotters, for instance—can travel as far as forty miles on occasion, there are few places a mosquito cannot go. They have been found on every continent, in airplanes, in submarines and, of course, in office buildings.

That complacent little lady in the elevator undoubtedly has been done in by an aerosol bomb or some janitor's vindictive vacuum cleaner by now. Maybe some busy executive idly puffed a cloud of cigar smoke in her direction and dropped her in her tracks.

No matter what her fate, however, there's one thing we can be reasonably sure of: With the luck of her clan, that mosquito's great-great-grandnieces will probably be flying over the streets of Manhattan—or its jungles or its desert, if such may be its fate—long after that elevator has come down for the last time.

This brings up one more thing about mosquitoes. With the wigglers' fondness for algae, bacteria and stagnant water, these never-say-die creatures can stand pollution even better than we can. And that's one more point for the mosquito, right there.

The Way
They Look

Octopus

> Then the creeping murderer, the octopus, steals out, slowly, softly, moving like a gray mist, pretending now to be a bit of weed, now a rock, now a lump of decaying meat while its evil goat eyes watch coldly. It oozes and flows toward a feeding crab, and as it comes close its yellow eyes burn and its body turns rosy with the pulsing color of anticipation and rage.
>
> **John Steinbeck: *Cannery Row***

ORDINARILY you don't expect much from a tankful of crabs. Of course, stick your finger down among them and you might be sorry; give them a dead fish and it's reduced to a skeleton. Crabs can pinch, bite, run and swim—and that's about all. Probably nobody in his right mind expects a crab to fly.

79

But that's what the crabs seemed to be doing in that marine aquarium. Or perhaps they were climbing up the sheer walls of the tank, over the edge and out to freedom where nobody ever saw them again. In either case, every day the caretaker would count the crotchety crustaceans and every day there would be a few less. Obviously the crabs were going somewhere. But where? And how?

Then somebody noticed that the crabs hadn't disappeared entirely. Half hidden among the scenery at the bottom of the tank were a few relics: a claw here, a leg there; plus a body-shell or two, opened expertly as a connoisseur would open a crab—top half separated from the bottom half, and contents scooped out.

That last discovery did it. To the knowledgeable scientists there was only one creature dextrous enough for such a job. Somehow, an octopus must have been dumped into the tank with a load of crabs. Now it was hiding among the material on the bottom, quietly helping itself to a gourmet meal whenever it wished. The crabs weren't flying off into thin air at all—though doubtless they would have if they could.

So the authorities set about to remove the prankster. Carefully checking each corner of the tank, they stood ready to collar the culprit when they flushed him out.

But—no octopus. Every potential hiding place, and those that weren't so potential, drew a blank. Knowing the capacity of the octopus to change color and pattern to match its surroundings, the caretakers paid special attention to the bottom debris, thinking their quarry might be hiding in plain sight. Still no octopus.

Yet all those crabs hadn't just up and died. They hadn't had an underwater war, either. There just had to be an octopus. But where?

The answer lay in a nearby tank. Nestled in its cubbyhole, gazing innocently out on the world, was the ancient nemesis of crabdom. Its body gently rising and falling as it passed water over its gills and let it out through its siphon, the octopus quietly breathed in its almost-human way and quietly looked with its almost-human eyes. Obviously nobody could ever suspect such a guileless creature. Besides, how would it ever get from this tank to that one?

A little sleuthing on the part of its human keepers solved the mystery. The octopus waited until the aquarium had closed down for the night, and then it simply went out for supper.

Reaching up above the surface of the water where it stayed so peacefully all day, the octopus clamped a few suckers of an arm or two to the glass of its aquarium. Even as it hauled itself up, more suckers were reaching forward for a fresh grasp, and so it flowed up to the top of the glass. Then down the other side, over to the crab tank, up the glass and down again—and the delightful bonanza of an after-hours feast. A hasty reshuffling of living quarters put a stop to the carnage among the crabs.

But that's the way it is with the octopus. It not only has the ability to size up an unusual situation, but it has the capacity to do something about it. Many scientists, after watching the behavior of this eight-armed cousin of the lowly clam, have come to the conclusion that it is about the most intelligent creature in the entire invertebrate world. And that's taking into account the marvelous actions of ants and bees, too.

An octopus can look at a crab through a window, for instance. Then it can learn to climb a platform, go down a wall, up over a hurdle and around a corner to get the crab. Yet the only time its food was in sight was that brief glimpse through the window. Of course the octopus doesn't do this perfectly on the first try, or even the second. But it can learn.

I first became acquainted with these baggy-bodied molluscs when I was stationed in Europe during World War II. On a weekend pass to the Riviera, I met a gentleman who showed me his trained octopus.

"Jacques" was medium-sized for an octopus—about eight inches in spread from the tip of one tentacle to the other. He was in a little pool about the size and depth of a bathtub. He took his ease beneath a sheltering stone which, his master informed me, the clever creature had placed to suit his own need. The water of the pool was changed daily by the tide.

"He likes crabs and shrimps better than fish," my host said, "but right now fish is all I have. Shrimp is expensive. That is why you see the money on the bottom of the pool."

I had already noted a number of coins in the water. My host soon explained it all to me. It seemed that Jacques preferred crustaceans, but he would take fish—apparently part of the performance I was about to witness—if he thought there would be a chance for crabs or shrimp in the future. Or so the man assured me. Here was where those francs and centimes entered into the picture: they helped buy food for clever Jacques. And for his still more clever master.

Dutifully taking a coin from my pocket, I tossed it into the water. The result was surprising. As if he had been yanked out of his cave by a string—he didn't merely crawl, he jet-propelled himself with his siphon—Jacques shot across to the other side of the pool. There, in the shallows, was a small earthenware jar that I hadn't noticed, but Jacques obviously was fully aware of it. Before my astonished eyes, he swarmed over the jar. In an instant I saw its wooden cover slip aside. In another instant the octopus had extracted a bit of food and rocketed back to his den.

It had happened so fast that the coin had scarcely settled to the bottom. Jacques, enriched by about twenty cents, settled down in his cubbyhole to enjoy his one-franc meal. "See how he thanks you," said his master expansively as he removed the little food crock from the water. "Indeed, we both thank you."

It was well worth the money to me. In fact, when Jacques had finished his tidbit, I tossed in another franc—as much to grease his owner's palm as to see Jacques go through the performance again. I wanted to know just how the whole affair was managed. Casually replenishing the container from which Jacques had extracted his second treat, the man seemed happy to oblige.

"I wait until you are ready to throw the coin," he admitted. "Then I place the jar in the water—like this. And Jacques gets his fish."

But this third time the octopus made no motion to claim his reward. He just sat there, contemplating the scene. In answer to my question, Jacques' keeper shrugged. "Well, mon ami, this octopus knows that food costs money. And he does not work for nothing."

So in went another of my coins. And the instant it hit the water Jacques dashed out and opened the jar.

Of course! He'd been trained to visit his food jar only on the splash of something tossed into the pool.

I thanked my host. "Oh, by the way," I asked, as I turned to go, "are there many people as curious about animal behavior as I am—wondering how it's done, and all?"

My vest-pocket Barnum smiled. "All of them, monsieur," he said.

But doing tricks at the splash of a coin is only a sideline for an octopus. Its everyday antics are just as interesting. An octopus in its undersea cavern—alert, watchful, ready to act in an instant—is a whole bag of tricks in itself.

It is hard to believe that this hair-trigger creature is a true mollusc. It seems impossible that it is even remotely related to a slowpoke like the snail. It is harder still to relate it to the

oyster, with the oyster having two shells and an inability to do little more than just sit there on some tide-washed rock. Still, the octopus shares many things in common with the rest of the molluscs: they're all built around the same plan. They are basically a soft body surrounded by a remarkable membrane, the mantle. Locomotion, be it great or small, is usually accomplished by a mass of muscle, or foot.

The foot of a snail is the broad, flat sole on which it glides. Many of its body organs are hidden up under the mantle, where they are protected by the mantle's limy secretion, the shell. Some of the organs, however, extend down into the foot. Hence the class name of the snail, Gastropoda—literally, "stomach-footed." The foot of a clam or oyster, scarcely discernible as it languishes on your plate along with the tartar sauce, is shaped like the blade of a hatchet; hence Pelecypoda —literally, "hatchet-footed."

The octopus—as do the squid and cuttlefish, also belonging to the Cephalopoda, or "head-footed"—has the foot broken into a circle of tentacles surrounding the mouth with its parrotlike beak. Behind the mouth of a cephalopod are those arresting eyes, and beyond them is the body proper. The dome-shaped "head" of the octopus really contains the stomach and other organs.

Except for the hard beak, the body of an octopus is soft and baggy, with little support beyond its natural buoyancy in water. Thus the octopus hides in some cave or den. Squid and cuttlefish have a simple internal stiffening structure. Called the "pen" in the squid, this device looks something like a slender arrowhead made of clear plastic. In the cuttlefish it is white and chalky when dried—the familiar "cuttlebone" you give to your parakeet or canary. Perhaps the greater toughness of their bodies is responsible for the pugnacity of many squids.

The chambered nautilus, another cephalopod, looks as if it

really belonged with the snails, because it has a many-partitioned shell within which the animal lives. Most of the rest of the group, though, have the soft body surrounded by that mantle, which is tough and muscular.

A large opening in the mantle admits water to flow over the gills. The outflow takes place through the slender, flexible siphon. For jet propulsion the animal merely contracts the mantle swiftly, squirting water through its siphon. By pointing the siphon forward or backward the creature can dart as it chooses to the opposite direction.

If the octopus stuck to jet-propulsion, it would doubtless be greeted with far less apprehension. But it insists on flowing along on those eight legs, which resemble so many serpents. And those suction discs—sometimes more than a hundred of them per leg, depending on the species—are such an unorthodox way of taking hold of things. Add those startling eyes, complete with iris, pupil, lens and even eyelids in some kinds. Top it all off with a saggy body that often drapes itself like an underwater beret, and you've got a creature that *must* be from another world. Hence the octopus's common nickname: Devilfish.

Probably the average crab couldn't agree more heartily with that name—if crabs could agree with anything. Jetting out from its lair to seize a crab, the octopus descends on it in a smother of arms and suckers and parrotlike beak. Within minutes the cantankerous crustacean is nipped to pieces by the beak and reduced to deviled crab. Inedible fragments are discarded on the junk pile that steadily builds up at the entrance to the den.

So expert is the octopus at extracting food from shelled molluscs that its underwater front lawn is a favorite spot for collectors. The octopus removes the occupant of the shell and tosses the empty case away intact.

Yet the octopus is more than a litterbug. All those leftovers on the front step do their bit for the owner. Fish and other small creatures, attracted by the sight and the lingering smells that doubtless waft through the water, venture too close—and become a part of the welcome mat themselves. In addition, as the octopus rests within its little cave, it often has an arm stretching out and curled about the debris. If an enemy threatens, the octopus jumps backward, scooping an armload of shells into the entrance as it goes.

This hasty retreat can occur whenever it feels threatened. Octopus flesh is good eating, as most residents of the Old World—and many of the New—agree. Dried, broiled, fried, or baked, it has a fine flavor that reminds me of scallops. There are also a number of ocean denizens that will happily take it without any special preparation at all: sharks, turtles, sea bass, barracuda, and the octopus's special foe, the moray eel.

A clumsy shark might be readily foiled by an octopus huddled in its cavern, but the moray eel is not easily stopped. It may be misled, however, for another specialty of the wary octopus is the "smoke screen." It bears a pouch which carries an inky fluid. When threatened or injured, it squirts some of this fluid out through the siphon. Not only does the ink interfere with vision while the octopus makes its escape, but the cloudy fluid paralyzes the moray's sense of smell. After receiving a good shot of ink, a moray has been known to blunder around for as much as two hours, even bumping harmlessly into the octopus that reduced it to such a state.

Then, too, there are those astonishing color cells. These are little elastic bags of pigment borne in layers in the skin of the octopus. Tiny muscles surrounding them hold them open, exposing the color; when the muscles relax, the elastic bags quickly close, like the drawstring of a purse. An octopus may be striped, checkered, mottled, or solid in color, depending on which of the thousands of tiny bags are held open.

OCTOPUS

By taking visual note of its surroundings the octopus can determine the color pattern to use. It might be a buffy-brown in its cave, a greenish hue when lurking among seaweed, and a spotted pepper-and-salt on a graveled bottom. Irritated, it blushes a dark red. Threatened, it pales instantly to a frightened white. An octopus I once surprised while turning over rocks on the California coast went through a whole gamut of colors as it fled over the stones to the safety of a nearby pool. The minute it slipped into the water it seemed to disappear—until I finally realized it had merely turned suddenly pale, jetted to the far end of the pool, and "reappeared" as a mahogany object in the shelter of a rock.

Apparently camouflage, ink screen and natural shyness have served their owners well. Even with their hosts of enemies, the octopuses number about one hundred fifty species. They range in size from delicate little creatures less than an inch long to giants which may reach nearly thirty feet from the tip of one outspread tentacle to the other. Generally the octopus gathered by Mediterranean fishermen or found along many seacoasts spreads only one to three feet. And, in spite of our unreasoning dread of the octopus—inspired, no doubt, by tales such as Jules Verne's fanciful account of a huge man-eater—the retiring creature seldom causes the slightest trouble to man. Of course a diver may blunder right into the domain of one of these creatures, which may automatically defend itself. Usually, however, it flees as soon as it can.

Most "octopus attacks" are probably the work of squids. These bulletlike creatures are found in almost any sea. They range from pencil size to great creatures more than fifty feet long. Squids, with their ten sucker-laden arms, have been known to attack boats, fish on the line, and even occasional swimmers. Most of the time, though, large squids are found in the open ocean far from any contact with man.

The shyness of the octopus is used in two interesting kinds

of fishing. One method employs an earthenware crock for bait; the other uses the octopus itself. In the first kind of fishing, the crock is lowered at the end of a long line. Then it is marked with a buoy, as a lobster pot is. A wandering octopus, dispossessed perhaps by an enemy, or finding its former home a little tight around the waist, obligingly snuggles into the crock. The next morning the crock is lifted to the surface, the octopus refuses to leave—and is hoisted right up into the boat.

The second kind of "fishing" involves a sunken ship, or the ruins of an ancient city. Archaeologists, suspecting that valuable pieces of pottery might be down on the bottom, tie a harness and string around an octopus. Then, when the many-armed creature is released, it heads for the ocean floor. Finding shelter in a Grecian urn, the obstinate mollusc refuses to leave. With a little gentle tugging—plus a fervent hope that the tough-skinned critter will stay all in one piece—the whole works is gently persuaded to come up out of the bottom muck.

As might be suspected, the octopus goes about its method of reproduction in its own individual way, just as it does almost everything else. One of the arms of the male octopus is specialized for the task. Known as a hectocotylus, it is identified officially as the third arm from the right—although every octopus I have seen has been such an active jumble of arms that you might make a mistake when you counted them.

Remembering that the body organs of an octopus are sheathed in a mantle which surrounds them like an overcoat, you can see that certain difficulties in mating might arise. This is where that hectocotylus comes in. The specialized arm has a flattened end, like a paddle. This end serves as a repository for little packets, known as spermatophores, which contain the sperm of the male.

The male signifies his intentions by a gentle stroking of the

90

female at arm's length. Then he transfers a few spermato-phores by his special arm, taking them from his reproductive organs and placing them in the proper spot within the mantle cavity of the female. There is no actual mating as such. Some-times the end of the hectocotylus is broken off—spermato-phores and all—and lives within the female's body for days or weeks. The male, on his part, may regrow the lost portion for future conquests.

The female produces a few thousand eggs, which look like little beads of tapioca, hung up like garlands near the en-trance of her cave. Here the female guards them constantly. If silt or debris settles on them she carefully cleans them off with a gentle puff from her siphon.

The eggs hatch in about six weeks, depending on water temperature. Then the youngsters go off into the ocean. Tiny little creatures, they wander from one cubbyhole to another, or squirt their way through the ocean waters in the universal urge to spread out as far as possible. In the process, they are in danger from all the predatory creatures that teem in the sea.

Yet somehow a few of them make it. In fact, the cepha-lopods are among the most durable of all sea creatures if you count the total time they have been in existence. Some experts believe they got their start three hundred million years ago. Back in the dim past the great orthocones, looking like an octopus in the end of a large ice cream cone, produced tapered trumpet shells more than fifteen feet long. The ammonites, somewhat like today's little chambered nautilus, bore ram's-horn shells which sometimes were eight feet across. And even today sperm whales, which feed on giant squids, have been found with marks of suckers the size of dinner plates, pointing to an unknown kind of squid perhaps one hundred feet long.

So the saggy octopus with the kaleidoscopic wardrobe be-longs to an illustrious and talented family. He even has blue

91

blood, by the way. Or at least it is slightly bluish because of the copper it contains, just as our blood is red with iron.

But of course all this makes little difference if you happen to be squeamish. Coming across one of these self-effacing critters trying to camouflage himself out of sight in some rocky tide pool, you're likely to retire hastily and leave him to his own version of hide-and-seek—which happens to be the name of the game with the octopus.

Bat

The bat has sharp claws at the corners of his wings. He hides away in sheds and barns in the daytime. The bat is half quadruped and half bird, and is neither the one or the other, a kind of monster. It is an animal not less mischievous that it is deformed; it is the pest of man, the torment and destruction of animals. Bats suck the blood of horses, of mules, and even of men, when they do not guard against it.

The Library of Natural History, 1851

IF you had to choose the animal with a face not even a mother could love, it might well be the bat.

One bat will have ears so big that they have to be tucked down before sleeping, like the brim of a floppy hat. Large ears are fine—look at rabbits and deer—but the whole effect is spoiled by eyes so small that they are all but lost in the fur of the face. Then there are the bats with leafy facial ornaments

93

which make the creature look as if it is chewing on corn flakes, perhaps, or trying to poke its muzzle through an old-fashioned ruffled collar. Add to these the pug-nosed, under-shot-jaw effect created by most bats, and you've got a creature as endearing as a Hallowe'en mask.

No, appearances don't do much for bats. But then, they weren't created for beauty contests. They have an exhilarating life to live, and all the odd appearances, all that facial gadgetry, are designed to help them live it. They are wonderfully tuned to their spirited existence; in fact, so demanding is their airy world that they often have to "warm up" as a fine racing car does, before they even can fly. And in their boundless energy they have made their way to oceanic islands and to all parts of the world except for the polar regions.

We human beings would get along better with the earth's only true flying mammals if they came out into the light where we could see them, and didn't seem to insist on living their lives backwards. They sleep all day and emerge at night, when, according to folklore, they communicate with ghosts and goblins and other dark creatures.

Perhaps you think we have banished such old wives' tales from our enlightened existence. Then, how about this question: Which is more healthy, day air or night air? Test them both in the laboratory and you can find no difference. Nevertheless, an occasional pampered moppet is made to stay out of the "bad" night air. Yet bats are able to fly around in it unharmed; therefore, so the feeling goes, bats must be bad, too. And don't forget, either, that a bat likes to fly into women's hair—no matter what the people in science labs may say to the contrary.

The trouble with bats is that we seldom know much about them. But to try to describe a bat is like trying to describe a dog. Your dog may be an eighty-pound German shepherd or a three-pound Mexican hairless. My dog, Rebel, happens

94

to be the result of a midnight arrangement between a beagle and a fox terrier—both pedigreed and neither giving a darn. Yet they're all dogs, just the same.

So it is with the flittermice, as they are sometimes called. Look through a listing of the more than nine hundred species and you find bats the size of your thumb and bats as big as a kite. There are bare-backed bats and hairy-footed bats. Long-tongued bats and short-tailed bats. Tube-nosed, broad-nosed, gold and silver bats. Fruit bats, fishing bats, vampires. Then in southern Asia there lives the lisper's nightmare: the thick-thumbed pipistrelle. Say it fast three times.

Assuming there is such a creature as a typical bat, a look into its life history uncovers so many surprises that you no longer will have to listen to superstitions to get your kicks. The real thing is astonishing enough.

Consider the shape of a bat, for instance. Think of the familiar Hallowe'en black paper cutout you made as a child. Bat wings had to be scalloped in appearance. You knew, even without seeing one of the creatures, that the scallopings were made by slender supports in the wing, like umbrella ribs. These supports are really elongated finger bones. There are four fingers and a thumb, just as in human hands. A web surrounds and spreads between them closely, like a nylon stocking you are spreading over your outstretched hand. Hence the scientific name of the Order to which the bat belongs: Chiroptera, which means "hand-winged."

Now suppose the stocking is a huge one. Spread your fingers in it, but let your thumb protrude through a hole. Then put your entire leg and one side of your body into it, allowing your foot to poke out through another, and lower, hole. Such is the wing of a bat—hand, wrist, arm, side of body and (usually) leg enclosed in a grown-together double membrane, but with thumb and foot free. The wing often joins its mate from the other side as a connecting tail-web.

When the bat flies, each leg may pump up and down in harmony with the corresponding arm.

Then consider how it flies. A bat on the wing seems uncertain as to just where it wants to go. It darts here and there, sometimes reversing its flight or stalling out in a steep climb. But appearances are deceiving. There's a good chance that some hapless insect is at the end of every one of those erratic dodges and turns.

As it flies, the bat emits a string of squeaks. Some of these are audible to us, but others are supersonic—at frequencies up to 50,000 cycles per second, or about twice the top range of our normal hearing. When the squeaks strike an object, an echo bounces back—right to those big ears and all that facial gadgetry. In some bats these devices modify the sound; in others they merely receive it. However, if the echo says "insect," the bat makes a quick change in flight—and there's one less mosquito.

If the high-tension little mammal had to listen to every sound it made—up to fifty squeaks per second—it would be hopelessly confused. So there is a little muscle which momentarily closes off the ears with each squeak. Thus the bat can concentrate on the echo. And, since the squeaks are effective within only a few feet, this explains its erratic flight. The life of a bat is a constant series of opportunities seized or missed.

I remember one night when I was showing slides at a children's camp. The auditorium windows were open, because the evening was warm. Several moths and other insects flew around the bright screen, landing and taking off again. Suddenly two Little Brown Bats came in the window. They flew in what seemed almost complete silence except for an occasional chirp. Doubtless, though, they were also uttering those high-frequency squeaks.

I took the slide from the projector, leaving a blank, brilliantly lit screen. As three hundred enthralled children

96

watched, the bats darted in and out of the light. Probably they had followed a moth or two through the window and stumbled across the bonanza near the screen. One after another the insects disappeared. Finally, after they had cleaned house, the bats vanished as they had come.

In spite of the contrast between the intense white light and the gloom of the rest of the auditorium, the bats hunted without a hitch. Their eyes, small but functional, had doubtless been blinded again and again as they flew in and out of the beam. Nevertheless the creatures were perfectly at home in their little world of hidden sound. As each animal could probably recognize the pitch of the echo of its own voice, there were no collisions, even in these cramped quarters.

Bats hunt mainly at dusk and at dawn, when the insects are most active. A bat catching an insect is as coördinated as a ballet dancer—and much faster. As it zeroes in on its target, the animal steps up the number of its squeaks, so as to locate the insect perfectly. Sometimes a nearby bat, detecting the increase in squeaks-per-second, changes course. If Bat Number Two happens to be closer to the potential tidbit, it lays out a navigation plan of its own. Then it swipes the meal right out from under the nose of Bat Number One.

Even then, some insects get away. Feeling the shock wave of an oncoming object, they dash to one side. Some moths have "ears" tuned to the squeak of a bat. The instant the moth detects the squeak, it drops to the ground.

Escape may be only temporary. Missing with its mouth, the bat swipes at its prey with the tip of a wing. Or it forms its tail-web into a scoop. If it has just barely seized the insect in its jaws, the animal bends its head down into its tail-scoop to press the victim against the membrane there in order to get a better bite. This all takes place, of course, in mid-flight.

Its hunger satisfied, the "butterfly mouse," as the Aztecs called it, hangs itself up to rest. It usually clings head downward by its hind feet, ready to launch into flight. Then, carefully, it cleans its body from head to foot. A bat is as clean as a cat.

On a summer day you might find these flying insect traps in any dark place. This may be under the loose bark of trees, behind the blinds of a house, inside your chimney or—as my grandfather announced with a yelp that took ten years off Grandma's life—inside a pair of old boots placed on the back porch. They even risk frying by hiding under the sun-baked sheets of a tin roof. And it's probably true: Most churches have bats in the belfry.

So sharp are the claws of *die Fledermaus* that the creature has been found hanging from flecks of paint on the canvases of Old Masters in the dim corridors of a museum. Since a good spot for one bat may be a good spot for many, this must be a bit unnerving for an art lover who steps close for a better look.

In autumn the bats begin to socialize in earnest. They congregate in selected spots—caves and abandoned mines, for instance—for the coming winter sleep. They also gather to insure that there soon will be smaller editions of themselves.

There may be thousands of bats in a winter cave, coating the wall like a furry blanket. With such togetherness, a female may be mated many times, though just *how* many is the subject of a continuing mystery among biologists. Some species mate before retiring for the winter. They go through a courtship ballet in flight, with male actually joining female while their four wings beat in a sort of aerial lock-step.

A fall mating would be fine if the adults were active all winter. While some northern bats migrate to sunnier climes, a great many species merely hibernate. To have youngsters twenty feet above the floor of a cavern when the female was in a deep sleep would be an impossible situation. So, after receiving the sperm of the male, the female simply stores it.

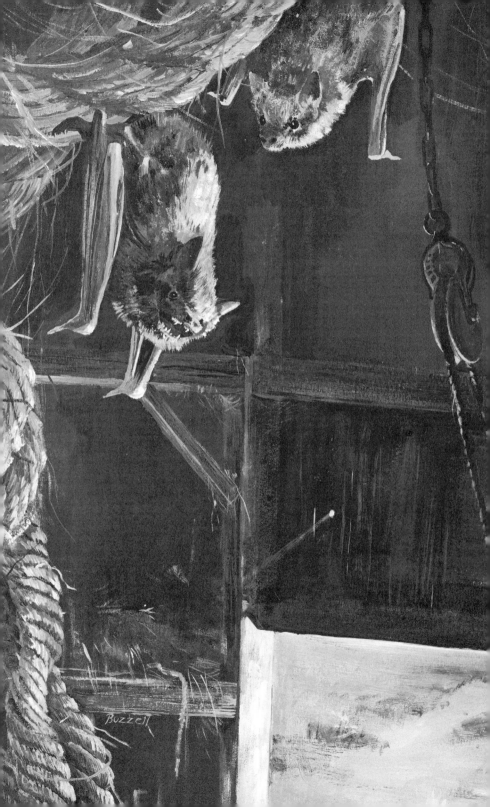

The spermatozoa enter the winter in the tiny incubator provided by the warm body of the female. Shortly, however, the incubator becomes a refrigerator as her lethargy turns to the near-death of hibernation. And thus the sperm is preserved until it is needed.

With the spring the egg is released for the waiting sperm. Seven or eight weeks later the youngster is born, even though the mating which produced him took place months ago. At his birth the mother may hang upright and curve her tail membrane forward. Then she delivers her baby into it as into a little apron.

This brings up a problem. The bat is one of the most active of mammals when awake. It may fly for hours in its search for food, and in the process it sometimes wanders as far as twenty miles. This would mean that the youngster back at the cave might get nothing to eat all night. Blind, nearly naked, and helpless, he soon would perish.

The answer is simple. The small batlet just goes right along with mother. Clinging to her fur, he must spend one of the wildest babyhoods imaginable. His mother dodges, turns, reverses and even does loops, but somehow the baby manages to hang on through it all. He clings with taloned feet, clawed thumbs, and backward-curving baby teeth. He even manages to find her teats—located about the same as the human breasts are—for a warm milk meal. This is like a small boy walking along the street eating an ice cream cone—only, here, the "cone" provides the transportation.

When I was a child I happened to be visiting a friend one evening when a bat flew in the open window. Immediately the lady of the house parted company with her sanity. She struck at it with a broom, knocking books, vases—and very nearly us, too—to the floor in her haste to do away with the startled creature. Finally, on a lucky swat, she connected. Dashed to the rug, the bat struggled for a moment—and

100

promptly split in half. Or so it seemed, for now there were *two* bats flying about the room.

This was more than the housewife had bargained for. Abandoning the broom, she scooped us both up, and fled.

When we dared to open the door for a timid look half an hour later, there were no bats to be seen. Our fissionable flittermouse had doubtless been a mother burdened with a nearly grown youngster. This state of affairs probably kept her from escaping that broom in the first place. But with the room to themselves both bats quickly found the open window. They left behind an unnerved female and two wide-eyed boys.

Mother bats may be hampered by the growth of their burgeoning offspring. When Junior gains weight, Mamma gains it, too. Finally the night comes when the youngster must stay behind. If he's not yet able to pursue his own food, his mother hangs him up at home. There he waits for her return from her night out.

Apparently there is little real family life among the bats. When the females of some species feel the press of impending confinement they may congregate in a sort of maternity ward of several hundred expectant mothers. The males gather in stag clubs of their own. This division is especially evident at the end of winter. At this time some congregations of bats may contain thousands of individuals, all of the same sex.

Those masses of bats which fly about in caverns and on television thrillers are often of a group known as free-tailed bats. Peg, the children and I stood near the mouth of Carlsbad Caverns one evening and watched a quarter million of them stream upward for more than an hour. So thick were their numbers that it gave the impression of rising smoke. They left the cave with a direct, purposeful swiftness—quite different from their mercurial feeding flights; some of them would travel twenty miles to chosen hunting grounds.

We spent another hour with the Park Ranger and then made our way back to the cavern. There were still a few slow starters leaving the entrance; we could see them against the sky. "They'll straggle out for some time yet," the ranger told us. "In fact, if you say here 'til around midnight, you'll see the first ones coming back while the last ones are still leaving. These bats keep right after the bugs all night until the birds take over in the morning."

As I watched those free-tailed bats leaving the cave, I realized just how important these animals must be in the war against insects. With most of the birds asleep, the insect hordes would have their own way through the night if it weren't for the bats. Darkness meant nothing to these little mammals. They found their prey, one after another, in a world utterly strange to us: a world where the creature lives at breakneck speed, ever flying down a funnel of echoes. Along this funnel are strung, one after another, clusters of sound. The great clusters are to be avoided, the small investigated and—on hair-trigger notice—snapped up or passed by.

A few years ago a friend of mine was fly-fishing at dusk. He had just flipped his line behind him in a back cast when the lightweight rod was almost jerked from his hand. "In a moment something fell in the water," he told me. "When I reeled in and looked at it, I discovered I'd caught a bat."

The little creature had been hooked in the wing. Open-mouthed, it showed tiny white teeth as it chattered defiance. "It sounded like a bird chirping," he said. "It was so mad that when I'd unhooked it I almost wondered if I should let it go. With those sharp teeth, I thought it might fly right back and attack me."

Taking a good grip on his courage—and the bat—he tossed the indignant creature into the air. It flew off into the shadows. Doubtless those thirty-odd teeth were soon back at their

102

regular job: picking insects from just above the water's surface.

Since then I have heard of other fishermen who have caught bats on trout flies. And always the protesting creatures seem to be hooked in the wing—not in the mouth as you might suspect. The conclusion is this: the alert little mammals have flown up to investigate this fuzzy object in the dusk, and at the last moment have decided against snapping it up. Perhaps their sonar told them there was a string attached. But, dipping a wing to veer away, they have run afoul of the whipping line—something totally unexpected. The result is one highly astonished fisherman and one highly offended bat.

All this fast living takes a great deal of energy. A bat may consume more than its own weight in insects each night. Perhaps this is why these creatures hang motionless all day; they are recharging their batteries. Nor is it because they are "blind as a bat," either. Most of them can see fairly well.

We had a chance to check their visual powers when I was teaching biology in high school. A student brought in a bat he'd found in the loft in his barn. Most of the class had never seen one of these creatures at close hand, so we put our prize in a large glass terrarium about six feet long with a heavy glass cover. There the captive's pinhead-eyes scrutinized my every move.

He could crawl awkwardly but rapidly, raising his body off the terrarium floor. If I drew near, he'd shrink back, or go to the other end of his prison. We figured the thick glass walls must have done away with the possibility of his "seeing" me by means of sound waves. But his eyes took over for his handicapped ears.

If there is a cold spell during the summer, insects probably won't be flying. So, instead of wasting its energy in a fruitless search for food, the bat merely goes to sleep. Many bats can go dormant at the drop of a thermometer. Their sleep is profound, but not as deep as their winter hibernation. A truly hibernating bat has an imperceptible pulse rate—quite different from its usual five hundred beats per minute. Its temperature is scarcely above that of the surroundings, its breathing at a rate of once a minute or less, and its blood flowing so slowly that a cut does not bleed.

During such a near-death a bat's oxygen requirement is reduced to as little as one-hundredth of normal. It can even be immersed in water for a half hour without drowning. With its tiny fires banked low, the little animal can exist on the layer of fat it has built up for just this occasion.

Bats hanging in a winter cave may become white and glistening with drops of condensed moisture. Disturb one of them, however, and its metabolism begins to rise. Within minutes its temperature has rocketed from perhaps forty degrees to more than a hundred. It raises its head and looks around. Flexing its muscles, it shakes the dew off its wings and fur. If you hold it in your hand you can often feel a curious vibration, like that of an electric buzzer. Perhaps this is the sum total of all the vital processes taking place in that tiny body. Within fifteen or twenty minutes the bat is off and away on its own errands.

It is hard to say how long these high-strung creatures may live, for there is bound to be variation among nearly a thousand species. Captive bats rarely take kindly to a cage. Perhaps they miss the freedom of flight; possibly they need the balanced diet of a catch-as-catch-can meal. At any rate, they seldom last more than a few weeks in captivity. Banded bats, however, have been found to live nearly twenty years in the wild. This makes the bat a Methuselah of sorts compared with a mouse, which is old at two years. Perhaps this is why most bats have only one or two young a year, while a mouse may have a dozen: many offspring compensate for a short life.

Very few wild animals die of old age. A bat hard on the heels of a night-flying moth may run smack into the welcoming talons of an owl. If it goes abroad on a gray day it may end up in the nest of a hawk. Once I saw one of these little mammals picking cockroaches off the surface of a supermarket parking lot in Los Angeles. Suddenly his good deeds were cut short by the well-timed leap of a tomcat. Probably the cat soon abandoned his prey, though: the musky smell of most bats is too much for most cats.

These active creatures need lots of water. The great skin area of their wings constantly loses moisture. In flight they skim water from a lake or stream. They do this by mouth or with that tail-web formed into a cup. Their sense of timing is so precise that they seldom are dumped into the water by scooping too deep. Such an accident wouldn't matter, anyway, because they are good swimmers and can usually make their way to shore. Unless some big fish sees them first, that is.

In a cage, bats learn to lap water from a dish like a little dog. They also will become quite tame, accepting mealworms and pieces of meat from the fingers. But even if some way could be found to keep them in good health for a long time, they probably never would threaten the parakeet and hamster trade. They do little more than stay in one place during the daylight hours. As a friend who had found a bat in her summer cottage wrote me: "We named him Mephistopheles and tried to keep him. But we had to let him go. He was just too *sleepy* all day."

People are always interested in how hard a bat can bite, their curiosity probably wrapped up in thoughts of vampires, Dracula and rabies. Once in the excitement of capture, I allowed a Little Brown Bat to get hold of one of my fingers.

It chewed away in frustrated rage, but it could do no damage to the tough skin. On more tender parts, however, it could doubtless draw blood. Since many of its relatives are larger than this mouse-sized species, it is just common sense to treat a bat as you should treat any wild animal—with respect.

A man asked me recently what I was writing about at the moment. "Bats," I told him, "and all the surprising ways they—"

"Bats?" he interrupted. "Vampires? Not for me!"

So all bats are vampires, at least to him. True, there are such things as vampires—three whole species of them in South and Central America. They hardly get as large as Count Dracula in the story, though; their body is more the size of a sparrow. But their habits are against them.

Alighting near a resting animal—cow, horse, chicken or man —the vampire pauses until all is quiet. Then, moving ahead on all fours, it approaches its victim. A quick nip with razor-sharp teeth flicks away a piece of skin from an area where the hide is thin. Large animals are attacked around the tail and neck; chickens in the bare skin around the face. Favored spots in human beings are the big toe, chin or tip of the nose.

Lapping at the blood with its long tongue, the vampire drinks its fill. It keeps the flow going by means of an anticoagulant in its saliva. Finally satisfied, it flies away.

That's all there is to it. Or at any rate as far as immediate injury to the animal is concerned. The anticlotting material may act on the blood for quite some time, thinning it so that the bleeding continues several minutes after the bat has left. This, to say the least, presents a startling sight the next morning. But no vampire actually sucks blood, nor does it fan its victim to induce a hypnotic trance.

Occasionally a chicken, young goat or other small animal is weakened through loss of blood. This, though, is not the main problem. The wound may become infected. Then, too,

106

the vampire can transmit disease from one animal to another. Horse fever livestock disease and rabies may be passed around through its tender ministrations. Sometimes the bat itself catches the malady; it may even die—certainly a walloping hangover for just a little night out.

An occasional bat of a number of species may carry rabies. Although apparently not always fatal in bats, the disease may cause the animal to attempt to bite human beings or other creatures. Hence any animal that acts sick, sleepy or unduly aggressive—whether bat or rabbit or cat—should be left alone.

Sharing honors with the vampires, though far less fabled, are the number of bats which find smaller prey. In Africa, the Far East and South America the false vampires feed on frogs, birds and even other bats. They sometimes hover like big hummingbirds, picking insects off walls and tree trunks. If a stray lizard happens along, they'll take that too. Then there are the fish-eating bats, which swoop low over a pond, snatching minnows from the surface. Their hind feet are fashioned like grappling hooks with strong, curved claws.

Unhappy indeed is the Pacific Island farmer who receives a visit from the flying foxes. His livestock will be safe, but his orchard may be ruined. Dropping from their daytime roosts in high trees, where they have hung themselves upside down like clothes on a line, these great bats go forth in a search for ripening fruit. They must be an impressive sight: the world's biggest bat, they have a five-foot wingspan. They have large, expressive eyes in a doglike face—they look like a chihuahua with the wings of a goose. Their sense of smell is apparently better developed than in most bats, and their hearing is correspondingly reduced. After all, why listen for fruit?—it's not going to escape.

Once they have located a tree, the "foxes" settle on it with a whirring of wings. Sometimes their numbers are so great that they break the limbs to the ground. They squeeze the fruit in their mouths, extracting the juice and spitting out the pulp. Then, having rested from their nefarious labors for an hour or two, the whole aggregation thunders away into the dark, to be gone completely in the morning.

There are many other fruit-eating bats scattered over both hemispheres. They are almost always tropical, as you might suspect, for such exuberant feeding habits need a constant supply of food. As if to balance them out, however, several bats prefer their juice secondhand: they feed on insects which feed on fruit. These bats sleep beneath the huge leaves of banana and palm trees, sometimes even cutting the leaves part way through so as to flop down and form a tent for the resting animal. At night they catch insects from the air around their homes, or pick them off the foliage.

A few of these remarkable animals even have suckers built onto their arms, like the tip of a toy arrow. Thus they can cling to the inside of a rolled banana leaf all day. Termite bats time their appearance to coincide with the nightly swarms of their favorite food.

There are flower bats, too. Some of them sip nectar, some prefer pollen. Others go whole hog and eat the entire blossom. In the process, visiting flower after flower, they scatter pollen and thus insure the future generations of the plant. Some kinds visit a single species systematically, like giant honeybees. They even have a long, brush-tipped tongue to reach clear to the back of the blossom.

Biologists have yet to find a use for all the paraphernalia sported by the well-dressed bat. Nevertheless the fancy facial adornments have obviously served their owners well. Fossil evidence shows that these mammals were flying around as long as fifty million years ago.

The array of oddities found among bats is sure to give man plenty of food for thought. The witches in *Macbeth* brewed their concoction out of "wool of bat and tongue of dog."

BAT

Anybody knows that the Devil has the wings of a bat, and Deuteronomy tells us the flesh of this animal is unclean.

Four centuries ago men used to rub the thick fur of bats on their balding domes to encourage the growth of hair. Their wives rubbed the naked skin of the unfortunate creatures' wings on their arms for the opposite effect. Bat's-heart soup made a fine remedy for a bee sting, though it was a little hard on the bat. And bat guano from caves has been bagged and sold for years as a valuable fertilizer.

Through it all the little *chauve-souris*—French for "bald mouse"—flutters his unerring way in the shadows. We may not agree with his choice of night over day, nor are we the happiest of beings when he brushes so close that we feel the breeze of his tissue-paper wings. However, as he squeaks along in stereo and in living sound, picking out a mosquito here and a beetle there, the evening is better because he's abroad in the dark.

It matters not, of course, that his complex way of life gives him an astonishing physiognomy—a face not even a mother could love. She can *hear* him, and that's enough. Besides, in all that darkness his mother can't see his face, anyway.

Snake

> The serpent lvrketh vnder the grasse, and vnder svgered speache was hide pestiferous poyson. **Edward Hall: *Chronicle*, 1548**

A GOOD friend, who shall be known merely as Mary, presented me with an ultimatum. "I've read about most of the animals you've had at your place, Ron," she said. "Some sounded wonderful, like that little fawn. And I've got to admit your porcupine must have been pretty cute. But I'm warning you: if you ever write a book about snakes, you'll be talking to yourself. At least as far as I'm concerned. I won't read it even if somebody gives it to me."

Mary went on to tell me she gets positively ill at the sight of a snake. Naturally, such a situation prompts me to tell the story of this perpetual pariah all the more—even if she refuses to read it. To me a snake is as much a part of our natural

110

surroundings as a rabbit, say, or a tree. And so here I stand, about to expound on snakes and bracing myself for the expected boycott of a solid Indignation of Marys.

The snake problem—if that's what it is—is relatively new to our world. The first snakes probably didn't put in an appearance until the dinosaurs were nearly ready to leave. This was during the late Cretaceous period, only a hundred million years ago. So you can see they are comparative upstarts, geologically. The lowly, limbless reptiles managed to flourish while their huge cousins became obsolete. Today there are about three thousand species of snakes.

When you get to know these slender creatures you cannot help but be impressed. Maybe not love them, or even like them; but you've got to hand it to them. Laboring under what we would regard as a terrific handicap, they have still managed to make their way over much of the earth. There are snakes almost everywhere except on remote oceanic islands or where the soil is permanently frozen.

They have achieved their success by a close companionship with the soil itself—or with the tree limb where they sun themselves, or with the water where they swim. Anything that affects that soil, or the tree, or the water is likely to affect the snake, too. Exquisitely sensitive to touch and to vibrations, it becomes a living part of its surroundings.

In spite of the winning ways of snakes in the natural world, almost every man's hand is against them. They are a full notch lower than a varmint—whatever that may be. And yet the truth about snakes is fully as amazing as the stories made up about them. While the facts may never overcome childhood fears, they may succeed in presenting any snake for what it is: one of the most marvelously adapted creatures you ever will meet.

Start with their peculiar locomotion. If, as a child, you tried to squeeze in under some object such as a sofa, or maybe tried to negotiate Fat Man's Bend in a local rocky cave (as I did; and made it, naturally), you may have some idea of the handicap of no arms or legs. Under the sofa or in the narrow cave you were limited to the use of just your fingers and toes to shove you along. This is only one of the problems that snakes have solved.

On rough or uneven ground a snake can take advantage of tiny projections, throwing its body sideways into successive shallow loops and thus moving itself forward by forcing against these projections from the rear of each loop. In addition, each of the large belly-scales, or scutes, overlaps the one behind it, with its free edge thus pointing backward. To glide, the snake reaches forward a tiny bit with each scute and presses backward, similar to the way you could inch along on your stomach by using your toes. With a hundred scutes or more working in harmony, the result is a steady glide.

Most of the time this method of progression is fine. But it has a drawback in that it's only one-way: forward. Having, in effect, no reverse gear to its belly-scutes, a snake can occasionally get into trouble. Such was the case one summer day along the little road that runs past our house.

I was out for a morning's walk when I spied something strange beyond the roadside ditch. A soft-drink can was jerkily making its way through the grass. It would lie still for a few seconds, then jump six inches.

Intrigued, I took a closer look. The tin can, it proved, was the embarrassing headgear of a very flustered garter snake. The reptile had thrust its head through the opening of the can, perhaps searching for shelter or for the earthworms and frogs that are the snake's bill of fare. The slender head and neck had gone in easily, but when the snake attempted to withdraw, the story was different. Now one of those scutes caught on the sharp edge of the opening. And there the un-

112

fortunate reptile struggled, a few inches of its forward portion encased in a hot tin can while its nether section flailed and thrashed and tried to back away.

Reaching down, I pinned the unhappy creature to earth. Carefully squeezing its body so as to permit the offending scute to come free, I helped it to undo its blunder. Then, as I watched, the snake wobbled off into the meadow.

Occasionally a mother snake, heavy with almost-born babies, may find herself in dire straits. Perhaps a hawk sails off into the air while she struggles in its talons. Perhaps some farmer's snuffling pig has turned her out of the soil for an impromptu lunch—for it's true that pigs do eat snakes. Under such circumstances, the frantic female may deliver herself of her babies in the universal compulsion of all life to pass the torch on to the next generation.

It is this tendency to give birth when disturbed that probably produced the fiction that a mother snake swallows her babies for their protection. The young have a running start when born, so to speak, and can take care of themselves almost at once. The myth contends, therefore, that such precocious youngsters *must* have fled back into their mother for safety: they simply couldn't have been newborn.

Snakes that lay eggs may never even see their own young, because they usually abandon their eggs soon after they have deposited them. When the youngsters hatch from beneath their sun-warmed stone or from the little nest in the sand, they are on their own. No anxious mother hovers near to swallow them. But a good yarn dies hard.

Another story illustrated by the floundering female concerns her tongue. It can do several things, but none of them is to sting. It is no more dangerous than an eyelash. In fact, an eyelash is a heavy club compared to the perfection of the snake's sensitive, two-pronged antenna.

Far from being strong enough to sting, the tongue of a

114

snake is so delicate that its touch can scarcely be felt. My garter snake had no intention of threatening me with it. Rather, by sampling the air with its moist tissues, she was able to learn something about me. Picking up molecules in the air on her tongue, she would transfer them to a special organ in the roof of her mouth. This exquisite chemical laboratory— known as Jacobson's organ, after its discoverer—would analyze my airborne trail. In addition to her normal sense of smell, it would tell her, far better than her brown eyes could judge, whether I was a living thing or merely a stone.

Had she actually touched me with her tongue, her information would have been increased enormously; then she would have got what amounted to a taste. When I had a portly hog-nosed snake as a boy, I could sometimes trick it into eating cubes of meat instead of its preferred diet of toads by putting the meat in with a toad for a few hours. Although Chubby's eyes told him there was no toad there, his tongue couldn't lie: believing his tongue, he ate his square "toad" once a week.

The process by which a snake eats is like pulling a tight stocking over a foot. First one side, then the other, is worked forward. The jaws of a snake are equipped with loose hinges, somewhat like the slip joint of a pair of pliers. They also have a flexible center cartilage between the right and left halves, top and bottom. Backward-pointing teeth hook into the prey and the snake "walks" its way into its meal by alternately advancing right and left jaws.

Here, too, a snake can move only forward: once committed to a meal, it must finish it. This is fine for only a snack, but if it amounts to a half-hour banquet, a new problem arises. The snake also has to breathe while it swallows. So, near the base of the tongue is a tube which connects with the lungs and, thrust forward, extends out into the air. The snake rests, takes a breather—then tucks its snorkel away and goes back to the work of swallowing.

After such a meal a snake may be logy for a week. Yet there is more to its life than just eating and keeping out of trouble. For all their reputation for cold-bloodedness, snakes show surprising solicitude in their love-making.

Most mating takes place in spring, soon after hibernation. It often occurs on a ledge or in a stone wall warmed by the sun, since a snake must absorb its temperature from its surroundings. Rubbing his nose along the body of the female and perhaps throwing a casual loop over her, the male caresses his intended. The female acts as if she couldn't care less—at first. However, as the male's suit gains favor, she may rub and loop right back, and soon, when they are entwined almost indistinguishably, mating takes place. Then, depending on the species and the climate, eggs are laid in soil nests in early summer. In some snakes the female retains the eggs within her body until they hatch. With such a viviparous (live-bearing; as opposed to oviparous, or egg-laying) species, young are born in July and August.

Each species has its own interesting life history. One of my favorites is the hognosed snake. Also called the puffing adder, it is a stocky creature—too stocky to escape many enemies. Instead, it has developed a unique means of defense. Flattening out to twice its normal size, it hisses and strikes at any offending creature. At this point, the offending creature—unless it's a human being—usually backs away respectfully.

However, if the sham doesn't work and the intruder accidentally notices that the snake's "vicious strike" is often made (surprisingly) with jaws closed, the puff adder goes into Phase Two of its little drama. Suddenly seized with what appears to be the terminal stage of apoplexy, it rolls about in a frenzy. Its jaw drops open, its tongue hangs out, and it rolls over onto its back—dead.

If the enemy picks the snake up it hangs limp, as a dead snake should. But then if it's turned over on its belly, the "dead" snake goes into Phase Three. This consists of rolling slowly over onto its back again. Apparently, as the great herpetologist Raymond Ditmars once remarked, the idea is that the only position for a dead snake is on its back.

Other snakes have equally interesting personalities. There is the common milk snake—also known as the checkered adder—which has been saddled with the delightful tale that it steals milk from cows as they stand meekly in the barn. In reality no self-respecting bovine would put up with such nonsense. Actually the milk snake comes in from the fields and brushland on a more commendable errand: to perform as a mousetrap. Able to follow rats and mice right into their holes and devour the young, it can do the job better than any cat.

If the three-foot-long milk snake is able to do such good work on rodents, its larger cousin, the blacksnake or racer, should be that much better. One of the unforgettable sights of my youth was watching a five-foot blacksnake enter a mousehole at the edge of a meadow. It got results in ten seconds. To the accompaniment of squeaks of alarm, mice erupted in all directions from holes I never knew existed. They leaped out, dived back in another hole, and leaped out again. That portion of the meadow looked like a field of strange, brown popping corn.

There is a great size range in snakes. In my corner of New England the red-bellied, ring-necked and brown varieties are found under logs and stones. They feed on insects and other small creatures that share their territory, and aren't much bigger than a good-sized earthworm. As one fifth-grader told me, presenting a twelve-inch red-bellied snake: "You can have it, Mr. Rood. It ain't even big enough to scare girls with."

At the other extreme are the pythons, the anacondas and the "boa constrictors" of the circus—which may be anything from a genuine boa to a good-sized king snake. Which of all snakes is the largest or the longest is difficult to say, because there is always the chance of a larger individual that nobody has seen. Nevertheless it would be hard to beat the South American anaconda or the South Asian reticulated python. Both may approach thirty feet in length, with a circumference of two feet at the widest part. Such giants, however, are rare.

Speaking of large snakes, one common belief is that the embrace of a constrictor must be some sort of long-drawn nightmare. The popular picture shows an unfortunate victim struggling while coil after coil is wrapped around it, spiral fashion. In reality, the constrictor can be one of the most efficient of all predators. Its victim may never know what hit it.

I recall seeing a five-foot boa dispatch a rat. The boa was in a large laboratory cage and the rat was released in the cage for the snake's semiweekly meal. I was about to cry out at such unnecessary cruelty, but my protest was never uttered. In one blinding move the snake seized the rat in its jaws. In the same split second it threw a couple of loops of its body back and forth over the rat. Even as those loops fell in place, the boa squeezed with tremendous force. Instantly all body processes of the rat must have stopped—breathing, heartbeat, muscular and nervous action. The tail of the rat scarcely twitched; it was dead, right there.

Poisonous snakes kill their prey with a venom that paralyzes the nervous system or destroys the normal functioning of the blood. The largest poisonous snake is the king cobra, which may reach eighteen feet in length. The American tropics have the bushmaster, an extremely venomous reptile whose length of up to twelve feet leads it to be disdainful of man, sometimes striking with no provocation.

The poisonous kinds are the ones that give many people the willies when you speak of snakes. In my adopted state of Vermont there are admittedly a few timber rattlesnakes—a very few. Most doctors in the area where they're supposed to live have never even seen a case of rattlesnake bite. But such is the human imagination that an article I once wrote about all of our local snakes was delayed by the regional publication that accepted it, otherwise, the editor told me, he would have the tourist trade and the camping association on his neck. Lest cancellations start pouring in if anybody mentioned snakes in summer, he said, the article was held off until fall.

Or, as another example, a neighbor of mine admitted that ordinarily snakes don't bother him—at least, not much. "But you yourself have said it's theoretically possible for me to see a rattlesnake, Ron. And I don't know snakes well enough to tell the difference. Nor do I want to. So I draw the line at all of them."

The rattle-tailed cause of all this misplaced apprehension is a creature of unusual gifts. Not only does the rattler have the ability to "smell" with its tongue and "hear" with its body as do other species, but it carries a delicate heat detector as well. This is in the form of a pit between eye and nostril, a pit larger than the nostril itself. Delicate nerves in the pit are

amazingly sensitive to slight heat changes. Because of this organ, the rattlesnake is known as a "pit viper."

When a warm-blooded animal, such as a rodent or small bird, has been struck by a pit viper, the snake retires until its victim has ceased thrashing around. Then, guided largely by its heat detector, it "homes in" on its prey. The U.S. Air Force's Sidewinder missile is so named because it uses a heat-detector system to find its target, too.

The rattlesnake and its pit viper relatives, the cottonmouth moccasin and copperhead, have cousins in South America and Asia. Like most snakes the world over, they are generally peaceful and wish only to be let alone. Their young, however, are likely to be short-tempered. They probably have to be: they are abandoned by their mother almost as soon as they're born. Those tiny hollow fangs, already supplied with little poison sacs, can give a painful bite.

As small rattlers mature, their snippy disposition calms down. The distinctive mark of their kind—that rattle—develops a new "button" or segment each time the growing creature sheds its skin. This does not necessarily occur every year, so you cannot determine the age of a rattlesnake by counting its rattles.

To shed its skin, the snake rubs its outer layer off on some rough object. Usually the snake starts at the chin and moves forward, crawling out of the skin as it goes. Such a process usually stretches the skin, sometimes to one-third greater than its actual length. Then, sooner or later, someone finds the skin of a "monster" snake. And of course none of the reports helps a snake's reputation any.

People keep wondering how to tell a poisonous from a non-poisonous snake. In most of the United States, with the general run of snakes it's quite easy. With the exception of the brightly colored coral snake of the South, our particular New World brand of poisonous snakes are all pit vipers. In addition to having that nasal pit, they have a head more or less covered with scales, instead of the flat plates of the harmless varieties. The belly-scales, or scutes, of a pit viper are in a single row from vent to tail, while those of the nonpoisonous snakes are generally in a double row. The eyes of the two are different from each other, too: the pupil of the pit viper is vertically slitted, like that of a cat, while the innocuous American snakes generally have a rounded pupil, like a dog's.

So, fortified with your knowledge of how to tell the difference between a poisonous and a harmless snake, the answer is quite simple. You can try your skill on the next snake you meet.

Just get down on all fours and look him in the eye.

Spider

Spiders convert to poyson whatsoever they touche.
George Pettie: *Petite Panace,* 1576

I F I WERE to write the story of the spider in the fashion of the
modern novel, it would be a best-seller. It would have to
be, for it has the one ingredient that seems to rack up sales.
Visualize an Amazon who towers over the most stalwart male.
Give her a temperament like a prima donna's and a willingness to accept any lover who comes bearing appropriate gifts.
Then, for a spicy twist, endow her with a murderous impulse
to destroy her paramour when she's through with him.

This is how it is with spiders. Not with all of them, naturally, since there's plenty of variety, with about twenty thou-

sand species scattered over the face of the globe. Each species has its own story, but a great many spider heroines are true *femmes fatales*—and we often find an account of such characters irresistible. If the newspapers give any space at all to a woman who has murdered her husband, she is besieged by offers of marriage from all over the country. There is a little spider in all of us, I suppose.

Maybe it all depends on your viewpoint—but not just regarding the seamy side of the lives of these web-makers. What spiders do—and what they are supposed to do—in your own life makes a big difference. In some parts of the world your day is made if you meet a spider: the eight-legged critter is supposed to bring you good luck; only a fool would harm it. In the Far East the occupant of that cobweb in the corner has control over the weather. If you meet a spider in the dwelling of some primitive African tribes, you'd better treat it with all due respect—it could harbor the ghost of your departed grandfather.

It's in the Near East, though, that the spider really comes into its own. So delightful is its presence that a marriage blessed by its favors is bound to prosper. And what better place to begin than right on the honeymoon? A spider placed in the bed of the newlyweds is just about the most you can do for the happy couple.

In America the story is a little different. Somewhere between here and the Old Country the spider has suffered a sea change. I know a woman who nearly perishes if she has to stay in the same room with a spider—even a little one minding its own business on a windowsill. She probably would faint, if such a reaction was fashionable. Instead she turns pale, her eyes widen and she points wordlessly to the Awful Creature. The nearest male, of course, does the gentlemanly thing and she is rescued—too often by hurting the spider rather than removing the lady.

Yes, it all depends on your viewpoint. And yet even here in the United States where spiders are almost always shunned, there are traces of that old respect. When we were children we solemnly assured each other it was unlucky to step on a spider. A lot of people won't harm one now that they're grown up, even if spiders give them the shakes. "Don't kill a spider," says the old Vermonter, "or you'll make it rain for a week."

In my younger days the harvestman, or "daddy longlegs," was solemnly scrutinized as it sat on the back of a grubby little hand. Waving a slender foreleg, as this lanky relative of the true spiders does almost continuously, it pointed the way to some mysterious fortune.

Generally, though, the less people have to do with spiders the better. I've seen a garden spider empty a picnic table faster than a spilled jug of punch. A spider running across the floor is an automatic call to action. Peg and I spent quite a while after bedtime reassuring a guest who was spending the night at our Vermont farmhouse. Just as he went to turn out the light he had discovered he was not alone. We came to his rescue when we heard him flailing frantically with a slipper.

It is interesting to speculate on just what it is that makes a creature a social pariah from the human standpoint. Sometimes an animal is too much of a challenge, I guess. Take the wolf that interferes with man's ceaseless ambition to be king of all he surveys. Man wants the deer and the antelope all to himself, wants to move in with his herds and his flocks and be master of all. As long as the wolf is out there, untrapped and untamed, he is a threat to man's ego, for the wolf is one animal that refuses to acknowledge that man is the biggest stroke of fortune that ever hit the plains—or the mountains, or the forests, or wherever the wolf chooses to make his stand.

Sometimes an animal embarrasses us. Such is the rat, or the cockroach, which reminds us of the filth and slovenliness that

124

must be present for them to survive. Other unfortunates are those Ugly Ducklings whose looks are against them. To our way of thinking, the unlovely—and unloved—creatures are too scaly or slimy. They have too many legs or too few. They wriggle like snakes or creep like slugs. They are all arms like an octopus or all wings like a bat. It doesn't matter, of course, that they are marvelously fitted for their particular lives. They just don't look human, and that's that.

At this point, enter the spider with two strikes against it. Anybody can see that a spider doesn't look right; and it doesn't live right, either. A weary housewife can tell you this after she has swept out the cobwebs for the third time in a week. Any youngster worth his TV set knows about spiders, too—how they build weird webs in spooky places and how the Spider People almost overran the earth before Wonderman drove them back into space with searchlights.

One of the problems with spiders is the people who talk about them. A spider is often one of the shyest, most retiring bits of life imaginable. Yet anybody who spends much time in the country usually gets bitten by a "spider." Of course the perpetrator of such a heinous deed is never caught in the act—a fact that makes him a sneak, to boot. Yet when Junior wakes up at Camp Fearless with a welt on his arm, you'd better believe it's a spider bite: the thing came right out of its web and attacked him.

Probably the facts are that Junior has picked up nothing more than a mosquito bite—or the nip of one of those perky little green leafhoppers attracted by the cabin lights the night before. Some people are allergic to the attentions of all kinds of denizens of the wild. However, a red lump with a white spot in the center *must* be a spider bite. So the spiders are cleaned out beneath the bunks and ousted from the rafters and Junior has something to write home about.

But to get back to the prototype temptress, the long-legged

Amazon we started out with. Although it is impossible to tell the story of each of her widely flung clan in a single chapter, they do share many things in common: They can spin a web (though not all of them do), they feed on other creatures, they reproduce in a most remarkable manner, and they are usually capable of making a meal of their unfortunate spouses.

Take the ability to spin a web. Although other creatures have silk-making glands, few have developed them with the finesse of the dullest spider. Many caterpillars spin a capsule in which to change their attire from larva to moth. The "eggs" you often see being hastily snatched up by ants when you overturn a stone may be the woven cocoons of ant pupae.

Some black-fly larvae tether themselves at the end of a silken thread in the rapids of a stream. They turn into a pupa while still on their underwater leash, finally rising to the surface in a bubble of air and there bursting into flight as adults before they can get wet. And I've seen the little caddis fly—Hydropsyche, "the water spirit"—fashioning its net on a rock in a stream. The silken snare acts as a sieve to catch any potential edibles that float by.

The spider uses its silk in dozens of ways. Depending on the species, the silk may be an incubator, nursery, playpen, diving bell, lifeline, parachute, and shroud, in addition to the usual task of providing a supply of food. Some male spiders even wrap their brides in silk. If the male could think ahead, we might suspect this was just to keep things honest. Undoubtedly the possibility of attack by his mate never occurs to him. Besides, not all female spiders are this unladylike, anyway.

That silk is a marvelous material. It is far more complex than a mere slender thread gleaming in the sunlight. It can stretch like rubber, yet it is stronger than steel. It is so resistant to shock and age that it is often used as cross hairs in gunsights and binoculars.

126

SPIDER

Recall a picture you may have seen of a transatlantic cable, with a large exterior containing smaller cables. This, in effect, is the makeup of silk. Whereas most other creatures manufacture silk in glands of the head region, spider silk is formed by special glands in the abdomen. It emerges through tiny tubes, or spinnerets, at the end of the spider's body. There are usually six spinnerets, sometimes as flexible as fingers. Bound within them are often smaller tubes from which individual threads appear. Some spiders have a special perforated plate which pours silk out in a sheet; the busy hind legs of the creature comb this into a ribbon.

Not all spiders build a web. Go out into any field or meadow and you'll see many of them running over the grass, apparently homeless and getting along fine, even though as spiderlings almost all begin life, at least, surrounded by silk.

And right here might be a good vantage point from which to pry into spider behavior, taking the nonweb spiders first.

The eggs, resembling a few dozen tiny pearls, are placed by the mother on a silken sheet. If she is a hunting spider, wandering from place to place, she may spin a second sheet over the top of the eggs. Gathering them up in a bundle, she applies more silk until the whole resembles a small white marble.

She attaches the little sphere to her spinnerets. Sometimes she carries it between her jaws, half straddling it. As the sac of eggs may be as large as the abdomen of the spider, this becomes quite a task. A spider-in-waiting reminds me of a woman with a whole week's washing wrapped in a bed sheet.

Hunting spiders need all their faculties to run after insects. The problem of how to do this when encumbered by a load of eggs is solved in several ways. Some spiders just produce a few eggs at a time, with several broods a year. Thus any sac may contain only half a dozen eggs, and be of little trouble. It will go right along with the mother wolf spider as she dashes at a grasshopper. The bundle of eggs bobs behind a female jumping spider as she leaps at a fly four inches out in space. Then, halted by the silken lifeline which this spider trails behind her constantly, the whole assemblage hauls itself back to safety: mother, eggs and hapless victim.

Sometimes the egg sac is too big for such acrobatics. In many instances the mother just gets along as best she can for the two or three weeks before the youngsters emerge. During this time she may eat little or not at all. She retires modestly to a secluded corner, or she may parade her impending brood sedately on an afternoon's airing.

An occasional female of some species merely hangs her bundle on a handy twig out of harm's way. Freed of her burden, she chases and runs and catches until she is filled. Then, her needs satisfied, she picks up—literally—where she left off.

In most spiders the attachment between mother and egg case is far stronger than the few threads that hold it to the tip of her abdomen. As a boy I wondered what would happen to a jumping spider if I took her eggs away. Pinning her down, I carefully separated her from her sac.

The change was remarkable. She had been belligerent and full of fight before, rearing up on her last two pairs of legs and sparring like a tiny boxer with her two front pairs. Now, bereft of her baggage, she stood as if dazed. I poked at her; she passively allowed me to push her around. She was so limp that I wondered if I had injured her in some way. Relenting, I pushed the little ball of eggs back to where she could feel them. Recovering at the touch, she turned them into the right position and hitched them to her abdomen again. Then she faced me, peppery as ever.

Oddly enough, in spite of the precious nature of its burden, a spider will often accept a substitute. Take her egg case away, and give her something else of about the same size and weight: a bit of popcorn or a wad of paper. Hitching it to herself in the accepted manner, she may tote it around for weeks. Whatever the load is that bangs along behind her, it must be something like a security blanket.

The babies hatch in two or three weeks. Now the egg sac becomes a self-contained nursery. Many newborn youngsters would need a meal at once. Not so with spiders. Their formula is ready-made and built in. Each baby has a supply of yolk incorporated in its tiny abdomen; the youngster lives on this for several days. Doubtless such a provision is a wise one, for without it the fierce little babies, lacking food in those cramped quarters, would start in on each other.

As the little spiders absorb the concentrated yolk, their tiny limbs need to expand. The outer coat of chitin, with which spiders and insects are covered, is almost inelastic. Finally, under pressure of growth, the chitin ruptures. The top half of it pushes off, like a lid, and the youngster carefully hunches out of his old skin. He pulls each leg free of its covering, very much like somebody backing out of a suit of long underwear.

The spiderling may molt in this way half a dozen more times before it is fully grown. If it is a long-lived species it may molt as an adult, too. Each time it will leave a replica of itself in the form of a cast skin, and each time it will become larger as its cramped tissues expand before the new skin hardens. If it loses a leg it forms a new one which appears at the next molt.

After the babies have molted, the pressure of those growing bodies forces an opening in the egg sac. Sometimes the mother aids the process. Guided, perhaps, by the activity in the brood-bag, or feeling a change in its lumpiness, she tears a hole in the silk. And not a moment too soon. With the yolk gone, food has to come from somewhere: already the stronger have attacked the weaker, and unless there's a chance for them to spread out, only one spiderling will be left.

If the spiders are of a web-building species, their egg sac will have been hanging in a nearby corner. Now the youngsters emerge into their aerial kindergarten. The mass of them looks like a miniature buffy-white star cluster as they space themselves far enough apart to get along together. Then, when mother snares a fly or a grasshopper, everybody joins in the feast. Or they may get their meal secondhand, imbibing from a drop of predigested food at the mother's mouth.

Some spiders string a few strands away from the main web in a nearby bush at this point. The youngsters transfer to this basic framework. They embellish it with tiny threads of their own as their silk glands begin to function. If this juvenile network happens to be located in a favorable spot, dinner in the form of mosquitoes and gnats will not be long in arriving. Otherwise the strictly practical laws of nature come into play: the spiders chase each other away or winnow each other down until there is enough food to go around.

A different approach to the food problem is used by the wolf spiders. These are swift, hairy creatures ranging in body size from buckshot to ping-pong balls. After the young of these hunting spiders have hatched they climb onto the back and abdomen of their mother. There they cling to the bristles and hairs of her legs and body, riding piggyback as she goes about her affairs. When she runs down a meal, they share with her.

Two years ago a small boy brought me a wolf spider he had found in East Montpelier. She carried about two dozen youngsters on her back, as near as I could count. I put her in a large terrarium where I could watch her for a couple of days. Then I discovered something I hadn't known about these creatures. Although the spider usually had two dozen passengers, sometimes it was only eighteen or twenty, for an occasional youngster lost its hold and tumbled off. However, wolf spiders have good eyesight and the baby soon found its way back on the merry-go-round. Outside in its real life, though, it would have been left behind for good. Perhaps it

130

could have eked out a living at the expense of tiny insects and mites. More likely, since it wasn't ready to seek its own fortune, it would have been lost forever.

Although wolf spiders can see as far as ten inches—which makes them practically champions in the otherwise nearsighted spider world—there may be a case of mistaken identity. One female may spring on another female, with usually a tussle and a parting by mutual consent. But when both females are burdened with young they may be overly quarrelsome. Then there is a duel to the death. The two females dash at each other, legs flying, scattering babies all over the battlefield. With each new clash of these eight-legged steeds, a few more riders are unseated.

At last when one of the females is victorious, and things slow down, her youngsters hasten to their accustomed places. Not to be outdone, the newly orphaned young climb aboard, too. Their foster mother accepts them without question. Everybody moves around to make room, and the heavily laden victor staggers off in dubious triumph.

Young spiders look much like their parents. Their colors may be different: stripes, bands and spots instead of the more solid hues of most adults. Otherwise they are just spiders in miniature, with eight legs, eight eyes arranged on the front of the head like spotlights, and a body made of two main sections.

"The front section of a spider," wrote one of my high school students on a test paper, "is a combined head and chest. It is like a person down to the belt, with his legs up there too."

This, roughly, gives a good description of a spider's cephalothorax. Not only is it a "head and chest," but it serves as an attachment for all eight legs. It has a few extra appendages in the mouth region as well. Among these are two jointed structures, the palps, which project forward like a fifth pair of legs. Beneath them are the two chelicerae, or fangs, with a jointed hypodermic needle at the tip of each. Under these are the twin maxillae—more jointed, leglike mouth-parts. They serve as jaws, working sideways.

The abdomen lacks any appendages other than those spinnerets, and is attached to the forward half of the spider by a slender waist. The abdomen contains most of the vital organs including, in many species, a double set of breathing apparatus. One set is the book lungs, whose name describes their shape and whose thin "leaves" absorb oxygen from the air. There are also openings of the tracheae—passages that lead to the interior and carry air to remote parts of the body like pneumatic tubes in a big department store.

Tracheae are present in insects, too. Having said this, I suppose I had better mark the difference between insects and spiders. Insects have six legs as adults, instead of eight. Their bodies are in three divisions, from which we get their scientific name for the class: Insecta, meaning "in sections." These three sections are head, thorax and abdomen. Flies and beetles are insects. Spiders, mites and scorpions are arachnids, the term coming from the class name, Arachnida (meaning "the spider-like ones"—which doesn't help at all).

Thus when people ask me why a spider isn't an insect, I have a vague feeling of being trapped. "It's not an insect," I begin bravely, "because—well, because it's a spider. An arachnid."

They nod vaguely. "Oh, I see," they say politely, even though they don't see at all.

When the youngsters have matured a bit they travel off on their own. This may be only a simple wandering to the nearest convenient spot—another crotch in the same tree, or the next tuft of grass. On the other hand, some species of spiderlings may embark on a voyage so surprising that for

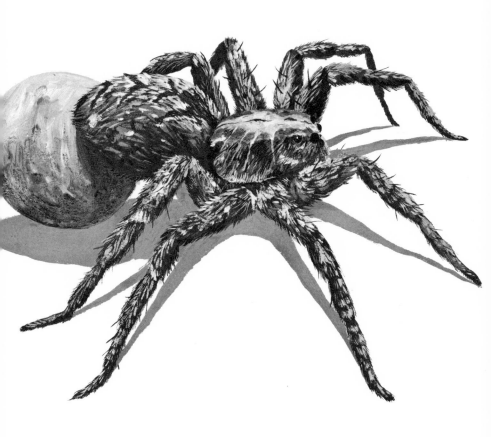

centuries it was thought that the little creatures had some secret powers of flight.

Climbing up on a twig, a grass blade or a fencepost, the youngster elevates its abdomen as high as possible. It pulls a bit of silk thread from its spinnerets. The wind catches the thread, pulling it out farther. The spider pays out the thread as fast as the air currents will take it. Finally, when the tug of the wind is strong enough, the spiderling lets go of his support and goes sailing off with the breeze.

It may take less time for this to happen than it does to tell about it. A sunny day with rising air currents can whip enough silk out of a spider to lift the tiny creature the instant it reaches the end of its climb up the stalk. You can see this happen on almost any August afternoon; the spiderling seems to walk calmly right off into space and go cruising away under the influence of some mysterious force of levitation.

Often the slender parachute catches on a twig or overhead wire before the spider has hardly begun. The little aeronaut merely climbs up to the new support and either philosophically begins housekeeping or sets forth a second time. If his luck is better, however, the warm thermals carry the tiny mote of life far out of sight.

He and his cousins may fill the atmosphere with the slender threads, lending a silver sheen to the air and softening the outlines of the distant hills. The old-timers called this time of the year "goose summer," probably named after the filmy webs which slowly settled to earth as "gossamer."

Those parachutes may carry their passengers astonishing distances. Ships two hundred miles at sea have suddenly taken on a crop of the little stowaways, and doubtless thousands of other spiderlings came to grief in the ocean around them. Rockets and balloons and airplanes have sampled the upper air and found spiders at thirty thousand feet. Snow samples from the tops of mountains have yielded more of these ad-

134

venturers. Carried by a fickle breeze, far beyond the timber-
line and there abandoned, they had frozen to death.

There must be a staggering loss among young spiders.
Swallows, swifts, flycatchers and warblers snap the little way-
farers as they hang helpless in the air. Dragonflies cruise back
and forth over a sunny meadow like animated shuttles, reaping the drifting harvest. An August noon that sees ten thousand hopefuls taking flight may turn into an evening with
nine thousand strands of gossamer settling to earth—empty.

Land-traveling spiderlings hardly fare better. They are
caught by tiger beetles, ants, wasps, birds and even other
spiders. And no matter by which method the youngsters
travel, they must find the right spot to make a living. Luckily
they have no way to realize the odds against them, so they
build their tiny webs and wait. Or, if they are hunting spiders,
they take up their hobo existence where they find themselves.

The web of a juvenile spider may be a simple version of the
adult's masterpiece, or it may be the nucleus on which the
final web will be built. When we bought our old farmhouse
we found webs which had been in the cellar for years. Some
were so thick with dust that they looked like saggy burlap.
Many of them were still in use until Peg deposed their inhabitants with a broom. Of course the webs were back in a couple
of days—little ones for small spiders and larger ones for adults.
Over Peg's protests I allowed them to stay, checking up on
them frequently. The little webs slowly grew larger as the
youngsters improved on their early efforts.

The kinds of spider webs are almost endless. Each web-
spinner has a basic architectural pattern, which varies a bit according to location.

The familiar, traditional web of the garden spider, with its
radiating spokes and spiral center, is a perfect trap for a leaping grasshopper or a dancing crane fly. The spider often remains in dead center, awaiting an unlucky passer-by. When

an insect blunders into the trap, the spider sways violently back and forth in the web, tangling the hapless victim further.

Gifted with an exquisite sense of touch, the spider quickly tells which of the spokes is nearest the victim. A thin film of oil on her legs and body helps prevent her from becoming entangled as she rushes toward her prey. In addition, while certain strands of web are sticky and coated with tiny beads of glue, others are dry and nonadhesive. She runs on the latter with the special claws that are unique to these web-spinning types. Coming close to the insect, she pulls loops of silk from her spinnerets and throws it on the victim with her back legs. Then she turns the insect over and over, reeling silk on it as one would wind a spool.

When her potential dinner is safely shrouded in its strait jacket, the spider gives it a quick nip with those two hypodermic fangs. The poison apparently has a numbing effect, and soon the insect is still. Then the spider punctures a hole in her victim and floods its interior with a digestive fluid that quickly liquefies the tissues. Alternately pumping and sucking over several hours if the insect is a large one, she reduces the insect to an empty shell. Cutting her meal loose from the web, the spider allows it to drop while she repairs the strands for the next dinner guest.

That delicate sense of touch guides a spider in the creation of its web. It lays down the basic framework—in the case of the garden spider this is the main spokes of the "wheel"—and works from there. Once started, the spider builds according to the previous strands, like a plowman placing his new furrow right next to the last one.

Scientists are impressed with such a step-by-step progression, and made an interesting discovery: the whole affair is like the workings of a little clockwork toy. Once started, the spider must go through to the end. Carefully remove most of a nearly completed web, and the industrious creature cannot tell the difference. It finishes what's left of its abbreviated web and stops right there. Spiders given a dose of the drug LSD apparently went on their own little "trips," concocting square webs, zigzag webs or wobbly creations that wouldn't hold up even their owners.

The ways in which the many kinds of spiders trap their victims are fascinating. One spider carries a woven net loosely between its hind legs. When it spies a potential meal it launches itself on the unsuspecting insect. As it hurtles through the air it spreads its legs—and the net—and lands on its victim like a housewife catching an agile puppy with a blanket. Another spider hangs from a twig and whirls a gooey bit of gum at the end of a length of thread. Several times an hour the spider brings back its sticky string, eating it as it hauls it up; any unlucky insects that have slammed into the thread are consumed too. Then the spider lets out a new string and starts all over again.

Look into the center of a flower, and you may see a crab spider, colored like the blossom, waiting to catch an unwary insect. Then there is the famous trap-door spider, which stays in the entrance to its underground burrow. If an enemy comes, the spider retires beneath its hinged door, holding it tightly shut. If a potential lunch wanders by, the spider runs out, grabs its victim, and pops back out of sight.

One of the spiders I used to wonder about was a certain kind that lives under rocks and ledges beneath a filmy sheet of silk. Apparently a self-made captive, it seemed to have no way to capture food. One day I saw it in action, however. A small cricket happened to wander across the sheet. Instantly the spider nabbed it from within by those fangs, holding it in a mouthful of web until the cricket was still, then pulled it right through the silk. The next day when I returned the cricket's remains lay outside and the web had been repaired.

Then there is the spider that neither builds a web nor runs

its victims down. This spider ambles up to the nearest potential dinner, and, without warning, spits at its victim. Globs of
sticky gum arch over the unsuspecting prey, trailing gluey
strands which soon bind the insect to earth.

Some spiders live in the webs of others. When a meal arrives, the freeloaders either heist the food off for themselves
or surreptitiously share the meal with their hosts. There are spiders that attack other spiders, too—right in the web.

A few spiders take advantage of the natural protection of
a nest of ants and live alongside these warlike insects. They
even look like ants, with slender bodies and with the front
legs held up as they walk, like the antennae of an ant. The
ants tolerate their odd roommates, and benefit by the spiders'
consumption of mites, springtails and other pests. Apparently
the mysterious disappearance of an occasional ant larva is
merely payment received for services rendered.

Diving spiders spend most of their lives under water. They
build submerged dome-shaped diving bells of silk into which
they release bubbles of air carried down in a silken cup held
by their hind legs. The spider lives in its submarine cavern,
capturing insects, tadpoles and even small fish. When prowl-
ing about for its aquatic prey the spider breathes the air that
clings in a shimmering film to its finely haired body.

One of the most famous hunting spiders is the tarantula. Actually this term has come to apply to almost any large, hairy
spider, for the real tarantula is typically found in the province
of Taranto, Italy—hence the name. When you were bitten by
a true tarantula, your only salvation was to undergo frenzied
activity—to "sweat out the poison." Such a course of action
came to be a dance accompanied by impassioned music and
known as the Tarantella. You danced until you were exhausted. The whole affair is so stimulating that you can get
up a Tarantella among those in the know almost any time.

138

SPIDER

Whether or not you have the spider is merely a minor detail.

Our Southwestern and tropical "tarantulas" are twice as large as the real one. These big wolf spiders look fierce, with hairy legs and body, and the ability to run like a streak. People are fond of telling how tarantulas can cover a saucer with their outstretched legs. The mounted specimen I have a few inches from my typewriter could do this easily. When she was alive, her legs covered my hand.

My tarantula was found by workmen unloading a shipment of bananas from Central America. She was brought to me in a half-gallon jar. When I poked a broom straw at her she savagely clipped it in two.

Knowing that spiders need water constantly and suspecting that she'd had a long, dry ride, I replaced the broom straw with a sopping wad of cotton. It was an instant success. She drank deeply. From that time on, her outlook changed. In a day or so she had turned into a fascinating pet. And, as my wife agreed while we contemplated the largest resident of our ten-gallon vivarium, a tarantula on the bookcase is unbeatable as a conversation starter.

Like most hunting spiders, she pounced on her meals. If I poked a dead mouse or roadside-killed sparrow toward her she ran forward, snatched it from my fingers, and retired to a corner. Then, working her meal over thoroughly with fangs and maxillae, she reduced it to a small bundle of fur or feathers in twenty-four hours.

I had our unusual pet a little more than a year. She never tried to bite us, and, far from being a fearsome creature, she became a neighborhood attraction. I was teaching high school at the time, and finally had to put a big Do Not Disturb sign on her cage when I took her to school. The students all wanted to take her out and let her crawl on their arms.

She finally died in July, while school was out. Perhaps some chemical in the laboratory affected her and finally did her in.

She—or rather her carefully mounted remains—must belong to the tropical American group known as the bird-eating spiders. Certainly she would have been completely capable of catching a small bird if she had had the chance. Some bird-eaters are among the largest of spiders, with bodies nearly four inches long and a legspan of eight inches. They catch lizards and occasional birds in South American jungles. On the other extreme, the smallest spiders are scarcely the size of the head of a pin as adults.

One of the questions asked unfailingly about tarantulas is how poisonous they really are. The answer is that their bite is about like the sting of a wasp. People have died from the effects of their bite, but people die from bee stings every year, too. A friend of mine was stung by a bumblebee as she sniffed a flower. She never recovered, and died a year later.

Thoughts of spider bites bring up the subject of the most notorious spider of them all—the black widow. Here, again, the creature scarcely lives up to its reputation. Black widow venom is more deadly, drop for drop, than that of the rattlesnake, it is true. But your chances of receiving as much as one single drop are almost nil. In the first place, the black widow has a body scarcely larger than a good-sized garden pea, so a single drop would be about all she could muster. Then, too, the retiring creature is painfully shy, and spends her life in hiding beneath lumber piles and in the hollows of old building foundations.

Even if you disturb a black widow, you're still pretty safe. She will huddle into a little ball in her web; or if you get violent, she may drop out of the web and try to run away. I made a particular study of this spider in the 1950's; there were only about half a hundred authenticated cases of human deaths

140

from black widow bite at that time; probably a few more by now. Most doctors have never even seen a case of black widow bite, although the creatures have been recorded from almost every one of the continental United States.

However, delving into how the black widow comes by her name is sure to bolster another side of her image. The shiny-black creature with the hourglass pattern of red or yellow on her underside might well blush modestly if she could read the first paragraph of this chapter. It could be the story of her romantic life. Or, with variations, it could be an account of what goes on over much of spiderdom.

Like other spiders, the black widow has a marvelous sense of touch. She receives messages through vibrations of her web. Usually the communication spells out "food," and she hurries to secure her meal. Backing down toward the struggling insect, she rapidly pulls silk from her spinnerets and flings it over her victim with her hind legs. Then she retreats to her corner, pulling her lunch up after her.

And then one day there's a newcomer at the edge of the web. It is less than half the size of the female. Instead of being solid black, it is banded and streaked with yellow, orange or red. The visitor approaches cautiously. And well he might, for—as if you didn't know already—this is the male of the black widow spider. If his intended bride is well fed and receptive, fine. If not, he may be the next meal.

Reaching out a slender varicolored leg, he tweaks a strand of the web. No response.

He tweaks again, stronger than before. Still no response.

This, in the spider world, is likely to be encouraging. Just the fact that he has knocked twice at her boudoir and she hasn't come swarming out breathing threatenings and slaughter—this is a mighty good sign indeed.

He plucks the net once more. This time there's an answering jiggle from the other corner. Wonderful. He places a

141

tentative foot on the web, then another. More twitches and countertwitches, and he reaches the side of his beloved.

Now begins an unusual process. The reproductive openings of neither male nor female are where one might logically expect to find them. In both, they are on the underside, near the forward end of the abdomen. With such corpulent beings as spiders, this arrangement would present quite a difficulty if mating took place in the ordinary way. But the spider has the perfect answer: there won't be any mating. After a search that may have consumed much of the male's adult life, and after this cautious approach which could have ended it all if the stars hadn't been right, there will be no mating at all. Not in the usual sense, at least.

Recall, if you will, the structures borne by spiders on the cephalothorax. One of the sets of gadgets above the mouth is a pair of palps—jointed organs that look like extra legs. The female uses them more or less as substitutes for antennae. In the male, however, the palps are greatly enlarged. Swollen, bulky and with all manner of projections like little fingers, coiled springs and hooks, they serve a highly specialized purpose.

Each of the palps of the male is hollow, or at least deeply grooved. It has a bulb at its rear, like the bulb of a medicine dropper. When a male is old enough to mate, he spins a special web on which he places a drop of sperm from his genital opening. Then, inserting the tip of each palp in the drop, he draws the sperm into its cavity.

Now the reason for the unique shape of the palps is apparent: they will fit only the appropriate female. The male discharges them in her genital opening. I have seen this strange activity in several species of spiders. Each palp is like a little hand, sometimes reaching forward several times to deposit its burden. It reminds me of scooping sugar from a canister into the sugar bowl in extremely slow motion, for the process may last an hour or more, despite the danger involved to the male spider.

That danger is just around the corner. Each discharge is accompanied by a visible effort on the part of the male. Apparently this has a quieting effect on the female, who remains as if hypnotized. At last her suitor finishes his task and jumps away. And with this, his mate is back to being her usual dynamic self. Generally she allows him to leave, but sometimes she swings into action. Then, unless he can make a quick getaway, he will be her next victim. And hence, on occasion, the black widow lives up to her reputation.

Some males stack the odds in their favor. One species catches an insect and trusses it up tight. Then he presents it to the female. Bribed by this arachnid version of a mink coat, the female accepts the gift—and the giver. Sometimes, however, his bequest has a hollow ring: he drains it dry before he presents it to her.

Another male, blessed with a ferocious spouse, adopts a different tactic. He chooses the time and place, mating with her just after she has shed her skin—while she still is soft and helpless. Some males tie their mate down with silk while the little lady is in a receptive mood, to give themselves time for a getaway later. Other swains impress the fair sex by waving a few legs in the air and running back and forth. Some of them drum on the ground with their palps, or vibrate the abdomen so fast that it makes a buzzing sound. This is doubtless the arachnid version of squealing tires and roaring motors —or bird song, or turkey strutting, or blowing up your schnozzola if you're a male elephant seal.

Not always is the honeymoon a brief one. Some kinds may live together as spider and wife all season. If an interloper tries to move in, the rightful mate may chase him away. Or he may just move over and let him take his chances. Marital ties are a bit hazy in the spider world; both sexes may take another mate.

Life comes to a halt at the end of summer. Many spiders die in autumn, leaving the world to an overwintering brood of adolescent youngsters. Others hibernate in cozy places: birdhouses, junk piles, and all over Peg's attic and cellar. If you look under the shingles of your house or peel a slab of bark from a tree in winter, you may find a few of these spiders. Some are warmly wrapped in papery silk cocoons. A winter thaw may bring a few light sleepers out for an airing on the January snow. With the sinking sun they burrow back down beside a weed stem or a blade of dried grass, to wait there for the next warm spell—and the next, until spring comes at last.

With luck, some spiders may live as long as ten years. But old age is seldom a problem for any wild creature. Weather and a string of enemies stand ready to do it in at any un-guarded moment. The black widow spider hangs her egg case in a corner of the web: emboldened by its presence she rushes forth to battle any intruder. But she may guard in vain. A tiny parasitic fly may quietly land on the egg case to lay a few eggs of its own. These hatch quickly into tiny maggots which feed on the spider eggs.

Small ichneumon wasps attack the eggs of other spiders. Some of the agile little insects even lay their eggs right on the spider itself. The wasp grubs feed slowly, avoiding the vital organs and keeping on the spider's back where they cannot be reached.

You may see the boldest enemy of them all on a hot after-noon. Flying right into a web, a hunter wasp sets up a com-motion which brings the spider on the run. Apparently having avoided the stickiest strands, the wasp stings her would-be captor, paralyzing it. Then she picks up the helpless spider and flies off to a pit she has dug in the ground. Packing the spider in the pit, she lays an egg on it, covers it over and flies away. There the spider, alive but motionless, waits to serve as provender for the new-hatched grub. Mud-dauber wasps do the same thing within their pottery nests.

Few enemies are more fearsome than the tarantula hawk. Two inches in length, this huge wasp hunts its great hairy prey, circling and flying at the large spider until it can harpoon it with that paralyzing sting. Then it drags it off to a nearby burrow, lays an egg on it, and covers it with sand.

Sometimes all the effort of these various spider-wasps, as they are also called, goes for naught. A tiny ichneumon wasp may accompany its larger relative as a jackal follows a lion, and also lays its eggs on the spider; then the tiny grubs feed on their larger relatives. I have kept mud-dauber nests from one season to the next—and raised nothing but a fine crop of ichneumon wasps.

In spite of all their trials and those tempestuous marital affairs, spiders have managed to hold their own for about as long as any land-based creatures on earth. Scorpions and the marine horseshoe crab, which are also arachnids, are older. But scientists believe that spiders have been around for about three hundred million years—which got them started one hundred million years before the dinosaurs.

So spiders are probably here to stay. No matter what the Miss Muffets may think of them.

A Little
of Both

Vulture

Vultures are very indolent, and may be seen loitering for hours together in one place. It is said that they sometimes attack young pigs, and eat off their ears and tails; but those instances are rare. It sometimes happens that after having gorged themselves, these birds vomit down the chimneys, which must be intolerably disgusting. *Cyclopedia of Wonders and Curiosities*, 1878

HE floats soundlessly, the sun warm on his broad back. From far below, from the land that shimmers with the heat, come the occasional sounds of another world: the bark of a dog; the noise of a tractor hidden in a slow-moving cloud of dust on a field; and that most penetrating of earthborne sounds, the crowing of a rooster.

The vulture hears these sounds, and doubtless they have

149

meaning for him. But they are muffled and unsteady as they swell and fade on the rising heat waves. Far more important are the sights on that multicolored patchwork spread out below. Important, too, is that vulture circling off to the south, and those two to the north and east. He is watching them as they are watching him. And beyond them are others of their kind, just tiny specks in the sky. They are all interconnected in a silent, watchful network suspended over the land.

The vulture's telescopic eyes pick out every detail of the ground below him. Day after day he has been carried upward by a rising column of air from the heated surface, and he recognizes every fence and bush of his little domain. That spiderweb-looking object is a dead loblolly pine. He has often perched there to get a better view of the honeysuckle tangle. The little trace of darker soil is where a tiny creek ran in the spring of the year. Now, sinking underground in summer, the creek yet supplies enough moisture to support a wandering thread of green which marks its hidden course. The vulture is familiar with the soybean field, the gravel road, the old cabin foundation.

He also knows that vulture to the south, suspended almost exactly at his level in the sky nearly a mile away. And well he might know him, for they were littermates two years ago. He is on less intimate terms with the other two vultures in his immediate neighborhood, but they are yet vital to each other's welfare. Guarding and inspecting the land below, they share in the common bond of a quest for food.

That food is carrion. It may be an opossum, at last "playing dead" in earnest. It may be a raccoon, wounded and treed by dogs, finally plummeting to earth long after its tormentors have gone back to their dooryards. It may be only a quail or a cotton rat lying there in the sun, but it is quickly marked by those piercing brown eyes.

Something is different about the weeds near the edge of the

road. There is a shadow that wasn't there yesterday. Half folding its wings the vulture slips out of the invisible column of air it has been riding. It approaches the suspicious shadow in a long glide.

Its descent is marked by its neighbors. Although vultures are nearly voiceless, this sudden change in altitude is as sure a signal as the scream of gulls behind a fishing boat or the roar of a victorious lion. Every vulture is alerted almost at once. The nearest ones, curious, begin to converge on that part of the sky vacated by their neighbor. This, in turn, brings others from farther away, and so on. It is just as if the network of soaring birds had been tugged from below by a giant hand, causing it to become like a great shallow funnel.

The vulture pulls up at the end of its glide. Now it is only a few hundred feet above the intriguing shadow. It glides and turns, perhaps flapping now and then to maintain altitude, for it no longer rides the thermal that sustained it without effort. The "shadow" turns out to be an animal struck by a car: a razorback hog which lies in the sun at the base of a clump of lespedeza.

The vulture drifts down to the stub of an old gum tree. At once his neighbors of the skies descend, too. They swoop gracefully lower, that six-foot wingspan bearing them in circles and glides. Finally they, too, come to rest in trees of their own.

They watch and wait. There is no motion from the hog. Finally one of the vultures drops to the ground.

Now it can be seen why these particular birds are called turkey vultures. The skin of the head and neck is bare, like that of a turkey gobbler. It is even red and blue in varying shades, heightening the resemblance. The rest of the body is dark brownish-black in color. Those marvelous wings are so long that they crisscross behind the square tail when they're folded. The feet and legs are less like talons than you might

151

expect from a bird that soars like an eagle. The feet are more like the walking feet of a turkey, though stronger and heavier; so the bird is well named.

Man, in his attempts to give human characteristics to animals, is often mistaken. Such is the case with our attitude toward vultures. That naked head and neck are regarded as ugly. The bird's appetite for carrion is considered to be depraved. And the caution with which it approaches its potential meal is of course regarded as little short of cowardice.

Actually, everything fits perfectly. In a very practical way, it makes far more sense for a vulture to have nothing around the head and neck but a few stiff bristles. Its food, softened in the sun, scarcely lends itself to dainty feeding—especially when a dozen birds are shoving and pushing. Neck feathers would soon be matted and soiled.

As for the supposed depravity of its food habits, we are far wide of the mark. The vulture performs a most useful job. To shrug off these great birds as being merely "important" is like the remark of a woman I once knew. She confided to Toscanini that his performance of a Beethoven symphony was "very pretty." She had made the understatement of the year.

So it is with the economy of nature. The vulture is much more than important and useful. It is vital and essential. The vulture eliminates a potential source of disease and pollution, yes. But more than that: with splendid efficiency it quickly returns minerals and organic compounds to the world of the living. Locked up in the body of a dead animal these substances might take months, even years, to return via normal food chains to where they would once again be useful. But the vulture, gathering with its fellows in reducing a dead animal to a few scattered bones in an hour or two, puts those minerals right back in circulation in the form of copious droppings.

So important are the carrion-feeders that they are repre-

sented in almost every part of the world. Where there are too few steady thermal updrafts to support the broad-winged vultures, their place is taken by crows in the more temperate zones. Ravens and gulls do the same job in arctic regions. The carrion-feeders are nature's garbagemen, it is true. They are also nature's middlemen. They receive the minerals bundled in a fox carcass or water buffalo or pheasant, and pass them out again with each new jet of excrement. They also distribute material in the form of shed feathers, bits of eggshell, nestlings which meet an untimely end and—eventually—the dead carcass of the bird itself.

As for the charge of cowardice, again there is a very practical reason why the vulture seldom attacks living food. Look for a moment at the hawks, owls and eagles. These raptors subsist almost entirely on creatures smaller than themselves. The powerful beak of a golden eagle makes short work of a stringy jackrabbit, but the tiny burrowing owl might spend half an hour worrying away at the lanky creature, before it got enough to eat. Let the jackrabbit soften in the sun, however, and the skin almost falls from the flesh. So it is with the vulture, faced with a cow or a buffalo or that razorback hog: if the bird is patient, the sun will do what even an eagle could not accomplish. This partnership with the sun is a main reason why vultures are confined to warm climates.

Actually, as far as courage is concerned, one of the constant threats to Southern heron rookeries is the black vulture. This creature, with little defense of its own, hops in to snatch the soft-bodied youngsters almost out from under their stiletto-beaked parents.

With the tough old razorback hog mellowed by the sun, the vulture applies himself to his feast. Above him, the network of his fellows has fast closed in. Soon the razorback hog is the center of a shoving, flapping, jostling crowd. Those strong beaks hook into a desirable morsel and the vulture strains to pull it away from the carcass, hauling with neck, back and thighs.

The birds gorge themselves. So efficient are their ways that the sun may still be high in the sky as they pick half-heartedly at the last of the bones. And so heavily laden may they be that it will be impossible for them to fly. Their gullets are crammed to capacity, making them so top-heavy that they must stand absurdly erect, like penguins.

When I was working at the Patuxent Wildlife Research Refuge in Maryland, we spent most of one day watching vultures at the carcass of a cow. After the birds had eaten their fill we ran toward them in an effort to make them fly. They flew all right, but one of us very nearly got caught in a downpour of ejected ballast: food hastily disgorged so the vulture would be light enough to take to the air.

This, incidentally, is one more way in which the vultures redistribute the substances on which they feed. When a vulture flies back to its nest in a low stub or on the ground in a remote area, it doles out food to its one or two downy youngsters by regurgitation. This is a handy way to provide food; and if you think of the difficulty of hauling a carcass back to the nest, it is the only way.

There are three North American members of the vulture family Cathartidae—literally, "I purify." Almost any open countryside in the United States may have its lazily circling turkey vulture, watching the ground below—and the neighbor poised in the air half a mile away. I have even seen turkey vultures near the Canadian border in Vermont, although typically they range south of New England and all across the nation.

Farther south the turkey vulture gives way to the black vulture. This chunkier bird has proportionately smaller wings, so it flaps oftener than its more buoyant relative. I have watched turkey vultures soar for an hour with no apparent wing effort. The "carrion crow," as the black vulture is sometimes called, seldom glides as much as half a minute without flapping.

The black vulture's lesser powers of flight are no handicap, however. A black vulture will land in the midst of a flock of turkey vultures, scattering them in all directions. If half a dozen of these belligerent birds alight on a carcass they will take over completely. Then the turkey vultures sit around in a gloomy-looking circle, waiting for what is rightfully theirs.

The last of the North American vultures is the California condor. Restricted now to a tiny segment of the California coast, the great bird has a wingspan approaching ten feet. This gives it a spread almost equal to that of the Andean condor and nearly as great as the eleven-foot spread of outsize specimens of the magnificent wandering albatross.

Once the California condor was a common bird of the far Southwest. It launched itself from the high crags of its mountain fastness and soared out over the valleys below. As with vultures the world over, it was alert to the slightest hopeful sign from its fellows some distance away down the valley. Hence the carcass of a bison or a sheep soon drew these huge birds from beyond the horizon. Man, watching vultures thus arrive as if by magic, assumed they could smell a carcass, but it was probably just the flawless operation of the aerial network.

When the settlers spread their herds of cattle and flocks of sheep on the open plains of the Far West, great predatory mammals soon availed themselves of the easy pickings afforded by this new source of food. This, of course, brought on the wrath of the farmer and rancher. He forgot that *he* was intruding on the land of the bear and the mountain lion and the wolf—rather than the other way around. So he staked out carcasses poisoned with arsenic to control the predators.

His "controls" have worked flawlessly. Predators, feeding on the carcasses, were in turn fed on by the vultures and

156

condors. The birds that escaped found their range shrinking as man cultivated the land, cut the forests, eroded the soil and built his cities. Now, almost too late to save even himself, man is becoming aware of the error of his ways. But the California condor, most likely, is making its last stand. An imperiled forty or fifty of these great birds are yet alive.

Condors and "carrion crows"—and other vultures by other names, as well—flap and soar and circle their way over the plains and meadows and deserts of the world. Sometimes they are protected by law, as indeed they are locally in the United States. Other times they receive something akin to veneration, as with the griffon and white vultures of Asia and Africa, which perform the tasks of burial in lands where cemeteries would subtract from desperately needed living space.

Their names tell something about them: Andean vulture, Egyptian vulture, king vulture, hooded vulture, bearded vulture. The lammergeier, or bone-breaker, picks up the larger bones and the skulls, flying with them to a great height and dropping them on a rock like a seagull with a clam. It was a lammergeier which, evidently mistaking the bald head of the poet Aeschylus for a rock, dropped a tortoise on it.

The Bible is probably referring to vultures when it mentions eagles. The ospray, most certainly not the modern osprey or fish-hawk, may have been the ossifrage—which, literally interpreted, means "bone-breaker."

But there is one name by which the vulture is never called. And that is a term—any term—of endearment. For in spite of the marvelous way in which this graceful flyer has become adapted to two worlds, he will always be, to most persons, just a plain old buzzard up there in the sky.

Pig

The common boar is, of all other domestic quadrupeds, the most filthy and impure. Its form is clumsy and disgusting, and its appetite gluttonous and excessive. Useless during life, and only valuable when deprived of it, this animal has been sometimes compared to a miser, whose hoarded treasures are of little value till death has deprived them of their rapacious owner. Thomas Bewick: *A General History of Quadrupeds,* 1824

WHILE the children were growing up on our Vermont farm, we raised a number of animals to help with the grocery bill. Our livestock enterprise included a cow and three steers, a hundred chickens and two rabbits that turned into thirty.

The steers, one by one, wandered over our pastures with

Daisy, our Guernsey cow. As each steer entered her life, Daisy placidly moved over to share her grass and clover and goldenrod. As each disappeared, she just as placidly accepted the loss. Since we also had a couple of tired old horses that had been farmed out to us for their waning years, Daisy could commiserate with her equine companions until the next arrival.

We never intended to make pets of any of our farm animals. I sternly told the children that all our critters were there for a purpose: to help support the food budget of a beginning writer with four flourishing young'uns. I frequently reminded them that those hamburgers and hot dogs they relished at picnics—and, thank goodness, never tired of during the rest of the year, either—also came from animals just like those out across the pasture brook.

Naturally, such objectivity didn't work—not with them, nor with us. We made the mistake of naming all our animals; and in so doing gave each a personality. It is one thing to fill your freezer with neatly wrapped pieces of *a* steer; it is quite another when those steaks and roasts came from Buttercup or Frisky or Chocolate. We learned the hard way the old country adage "If you're going to eat it, don't name it."

We had to give away most of our rabbits because I couldn't bring myself to do them in. I was forced to spirit the broilers out of the chickenhouse when the older children were in school and little Roger was having his nap. The demise of the steers brought on a flood of tears followed by a stony silence. Each steer, I vowed, would be the last. And each one was, too—until the freezer was nearly emptied and we had to worry about those supermarket prices. Then we'd start all over again.

But our system finally came to a halt with the pigs. We got two of them at once. Two pigs, we had been told, make better pork than one. Each pig eats to keep the other from getting the food, even though they're buddies when it's not mealtime.

Until we had pigs of our own, I believed many of the stories I'd heard about them: how filthy they were, how stupid, how gluttonous. When I contemplated Li'l Abner's pig in the comics, I figured Salomey was the perfect choice for a Dog-patch family pet—ridiculous and impossible to the extreme.

Now two pigs—and two heartbreaks—later, I realize that Al Capp in his New York studio knew a lot more about pigs than I knew right in Lincoln, Vermont. And here in Lincoln they raise porkers all the time.

We gave those pigs names, thereby compounding the loss when the day came for their departure. I should have fore-seen our problems and taken those amazing animals back the same day we got them, but I didn't. And although "our lives were filled with nothing," as Janice tearfully blurted out on the day the man who came to butcher for us delivered the fatal blow, we were by far the richer for their having passed our way. We learned, over the course of nearly a year, what pigs are all about.

Stinky and Winky were no bigger than a couple of cats when we got them in April. It was still cold at night, so, in time-honored farm fashion, we brought them into the kitchen for a few days. Letting them run on the linoleum, we were fascinated by the click-click of their tiny cloven hoofs. They were pink and bright and alert, with straight little backs and ridiculous tails that didn't know whether to kink or hang straight. They made contented snorts as they gobbled their milk-and-grain mixture. Finally they settled down under the heat lamp like kittens on a sofa.

After we had kept them in their kitchen nursery for a few days, the weather moderated. We put them out in the barn in a pen about six feet square. There we fed and watered Stinky and Winky and learned a lot about pigs. And, now

160

that we were in the hog business, we came in contact with other pig owners and learned still more.

One thing we discovered is that, for all their celebrated interest in food and their ability to make pigs of themselves, these creatures know when to stop. A cow or horse, let out on new green pasture for the first time in spring, may eat itself sick. And a cow loves apples to death. My father lost a cow once; she broke through a fence, wandered into our orchard, and fatally pickled herself on all the fallen apples she could find. As my sister confided to her diary, "Lucky wasn't so lucky—she died of a bad case of cider."

Not so with Stinky and Winky. Our avowed purpose was to help them create as much pork as possible before winter came around again, but when they had eaten their fill, they would quit right there. I remember one time when they broke out of their enclosure, rooted through a ripening crop of beans and wound up in the grain room. There they tipped over every barrel in the place, spilling horse grain, chicken feed, cow mash and pig food all over the floor. Such a performance could have spelled curtains for a cow or horse, but the pigs knew when they'd had enough. I found them filled and perfectly healthy, slumbering almost in each other's arms on a pile of empty bags.

In a way, this refusal to eat more than is good for them is responsible for the most familiar of the habits of a hog—making its home into a pigpen. Food left on the table, whether the food of people or of pigs, will soon spoil. When the farmer dumps today's rations right in the trough with yesterday's leftovers, his portly porkers have little choice but to eat the whole thing. Or sometimes—since much food fed to hogs is spoiled even before it is given to them—they push a lot of it aside in an effort to eat the best first. And, since pigs are by nature rooting animals with a built-in bulldozer in the form of that questing snout, this results in food being scattered all over.

It's in the field of personal sanitation, however, that the pig has been dealt the biggest outrage. We put a pig in a sty where he is barely able to turn around and then we point out how dirty he is by nature.

It isn't so. Not at all. In his way, the pig is as clean as a cat. One day Fletcher Brown, my neighbor up through the woods on the farm at the top of the hill, was helping us get in the hay. After the last load he stopped and viewed our two charges, now in an outdoor enclosure. They had an area perhaps as big as the parking space for a car. Their sharp little hoofs had cut the soil up so it was uniformly crumbled.

Fletcher looked at them for a moment. Then he turned to me. "Do you want to see a couple of happy pigs, Ron?"

Not waiting for my answer, he walked over to some hay that had been left behind. Scooping up all he could hold, he tossed the hay in with Stinky and Winky.

The change was remarkable. The minute the hay hit the dirt those porkers had a picnic. Squealing and grunting, they tossed the hay into the air, rolled in it, flung it on each other's backs. They cavorted like kids at the beach. They ran from one end of the pen to another, throwing the hay so high that some of it went over the fence.

They carried on like this for several minutes. Then that flair for cleanliness showed itself. More and more of their tossings were directed toward the southwest portion of the pen, where a corner had been boarded up for shelter. And soon they'd joyfully rounded up a nest of new-mown hay— dry and clean and fragrant.

They kept that nest, too, all summer. Along with their daily rations we tossed in an armload of hay once or twice a week. Not once did they foul their living room—and here's why I compare their personal habits to those of a cat. Just

as Tabby has a special box for his daily needs, those pigs deposited their droppings in the northeast section of the pen—far away from their parlor. Neither a horse nor a cow is this fussy, but whoever heard of "dirty as a cow" or "sloppy as a horse"?

The hog's miserable living quarters are partly responsible for another trait we have saddled him with: wallowing in the mud. With a thick layer of fat under its skin, the hog is wrapped in a perpetual blanket of insulation. This is fine in winter, but hot in summer. Lacking hair to any great extent, he also is at the mercy of the flies and other insects attracted to his unprotected person. A good slathering of cooling mud solves both problems at once.

Other animals, wild and domestic, occasionally take a mud bath. Nor is that all. Rebel rolls in a dead rabbit in doggy ecstasy, getting himself banished from the house. Your Thanksgiving turkey took a number of dust baths unless he was raised in one of those sterile wire cages. Perhaps the uncleanest animal of all is the chicken, sometimes sorting through its own excreta for undigested seeds, and often picking at an open cut on one of its fellows until the unfortunate victim is eaten alive. So serious is cannibalism among chickens that the farmer sometimes attaches little red plastic spectacles on the birds' beaks so they cannot distinguish the reddened flesh around a wound. Yet always it is the *pig* that's unclean.

Lest I be accused of trying completely to whitewash *Sus scrofa*—translated, sensibly enough, "the piglike pig"—I had better mention one of its failings. The sow does, indeed, kill her little ones on occasion. Sometimes she even eats them. She may roll on half a dozen of them, too, in some transport of matronly bliss. Animal nutritionists believe that she is more likely to consume a few youngsters when her litter is too numerous to survive, or when her diet is lacking in some nutrient. Thus she economizes all around. Others know that the danger of a sow's eating her babies is increased if she is uneasy or their lives are threatened. In effect, she puts them away for their own protection.

Nevertheless, that it should happen at all is a shock to many persons. There is no use denying it: the pig sometimes kills its own kind. Just like people.

Perhaps this is where the shoe really pinches. Pigs *are* like people—disconcertingly so. Their omnivorous diet includes almost everything, just as ours does. They suffer some of the same diseases and parasites. In fact, the so-called pork disease— trichinosis—can affect either of us: man, from eating under- cooked pork, and pigs from eating garbage with raw pork scraps in it. And the pig, under the conditions we impose on it, lives in filth. All of this hits pretty close to home.

There are about ten species of swine scattered over the world, usually laboring under man's displeasure in one way or another. For centuries the European wild boar, ancestor of our domestic swine, has been the object of the hunt. He has been run down on foot, on horseback, with spear and dogs. Like most wild swine, he is quick to defend himself, even pressing the attack with outraged squeals and slashing tusks. His distant relative, the little Southwest American peccary, runs in packs, and has been known to keep an overbold pho- tographer or would-be pignapper treed for hours. So formi- dable are the eight-inch sabers of the three-hundred-pound giant African hog that few animals smaller than a lion can best it in a fair fight. Along with the smaller (two-hundred- pound) warthog that looks as if it had a bad case of boils, the giant hog repels us in looks alone.

Perhaps it is this outward appearance that has kept strong the ancient injunction against eating pork. Perhaps it is the danger of trichinosis if the meat is not well done. Whatever the reason behind it, there is a strong religious and culinary ban on pork over much of the Old World. American pork travels under an additional onus with many European importers; we feed our pigs too much garbage. European pigs get far less leftovers—there just isn't that much food to waste. And so they get less potentially disease-laden food.

In the case of Stinky and Winky, we weren't concerned about how they might have been accepted elsewhere. We merely found them to be just what our more experienced neighbors told us they would be: basically intelligent, already housebroken, easy-to-get-along-with personalities.

Animal behavior experts say the hog has one of the highest I.Q.'s of domestic animals. In circuses or on television many of us have seen trained pigs which can run mazes, do simple tricks and tell the difference between a square and a circle. For centuries their keen sense of smell has been employed in searching out truffles, that underground fungus that is such a delicacy in Europe. Even the well-known squeal was employed by a zany musician in Louis XI's court. He lined up pigs with differing squeal-pitch—bass, tenor, soprano and so on—and elicited the semblance of a tune by prodding each in proper tempo.

So the pig—or, as it is called when it weighs more than one hundred and fifty pounds, a hog—has served man in a number of ways. Yet today, especially in the Old World, you had better not call a man a pig or a hog or a swine. The pig has long been the lowest of the low, and you're really upsetting centuries of religious and cultural tradition by using his name as an epithet. Often the only cure for such an unforgivable breach of etiquette is a knife between your ribs.

Our own porkers labored under no such stigma. After all, we had nursed them from active little shoats and they were part of the family. Even after they grew up, they somehow stayed small in our memories. To us they were still cuddled up under that heat lamp or tap-tapping across the linoleum on pink little hoofs. That well-known grunt, supposedly repulsive to the human ear, had long since taken on an individual quality with each pig. Stinky was several notes higher than Winky, and much more vocal. He also used to stand on his hind legs and peer myopically out on the world at feeding time. Then he'd squeal a delighted greeting when we finally appeared. Winky waited hopefully near the trough, and turned circles like an excited puppy when we poured out his food.

When the two of them finally went to their unjust reward, the children were inconsolable. It was like sending your own brother to the guillotine. All four of the youngsters swore they would never touch so much as a single sausage.

They stuck pretty well to their resolve, too. Occasionally we foisted off a few slices of bacon and once an entire ham. After all, hams and bacon don't really look like pork. Anything else, however, would be met with accusing glances and finicky appetites. For nearly a year any guest who came to visit was likely to depart with an unexpected package from the freezer.

When the last roast had disappeared, Peg and I heaved a sigh of relief. This, we assured ourselves and the children, was the last of it. There was just too much of a struggle involved. Now, several years later, we have come to think of pigs as pigs again, instead of Stinky and Winky.

But we will never think of the pig as "clumsy and disgusting," as Thomas Bewick, the great portrayer of animals, described him. No—we realize that he's an individual, with feelings and personality and interesting habits.

Which, after all, is what happens when you get to know any animal. Even an animal nobody loves.

Eel

> The eel has no sex, no eggs, no semen and originates from the entrails of the sea.
>
> **Aristotle**

I AM not likely to forget that encounter with the eel. Dad and I had put a chunk of meat out at the end of a long line off the dock. Then we had retired for the night to our little cottage, leaving that piece of Mother's pot roast to waft its tempting juices through the waters of the Maine lake.

I might have been dubious as to the value of something off the kitchen table as fish bait if I'd been older. As it was, however, I had a small boy's complete trust in the wisdom of his elders. So it was no surprise in the morning when we walked down to the dock and there was our eel. Naturally. All we had to do was pull it in.

It wasn't so much the presence of the eel that impressed

me, it was what happened next. Or, better, the several things that happened. Sometimes eels are so voracious they will hang on to a chunk of bait and allow themselves to be hauled right out of the water. In this case Dad had buried a few hooks in the mass of fishline he twisted around the beef, and the unfortunate eel couldn't have let go if it had wished. But that's no sign it didn't try.

Just getting more than thirty inches of eel up on land was a task in itself. Dad didn't know how firmly it was hooked, so he had to play his prize carefully. After he had tested it out for a minute, he let me have a try at landing it.

It was the liveliest thing I had ever had on the end of a line. While a conventional fish that size would have been a handful for a ten-year-old, some three feet of wiggle was almost too much. With more than a hundred separate joints in its serpentine backbone, an eel is all motion. While a pike or a bass is limited to fishtailing back and forth, an eel can whip that body into loops, U-turns, even figure eights. So while you pull an ordinary fish at least partially headfirst out of the water, you pull an eel approximately sideways. And if it can whip that body—sometimes as thick as your wrist—around a weed or a buried stump you're just about licked.

The second part of the show began after we had hauled the eel up a safe distance on land. Obviously it hadn't been able to dislodge the hook; now it tried to break the line. Throwing its body into a simple overhand knot, it "untied" the knot, by pulling its head through. As the line followed its head the eel clamped down and strained with all its might, trying to disengage by a straight pull. But the line held.

Dad found an old burlap bag so he could hold on to the slippery creature while he worked the hook loose. Then we tossed the eel into an old tub while we went in to tell the glad news to Mother. When we got back the tub was empty. Its erstwhile inhabitant lay on the grass six feet away. The eel had managed to swirl around and around in the water until it was able to vault over the top of the tub. Now it was engaged in wriggling its way back toward the lake.

Mother had been noncommittal about the subject of eels in the first place. Now she spoke her mind. "Anything that works that hard for its freedom," she said, "ought to go free."

Of course now, years later, I suspect that just the general actions of the critter might have had something to do with her decision. At the time, however, I regarded eels and snakes and spiders and such with juvenile acceptance. Each was as much a part of my young life as was a tree, a rabbit or a babbling brook. And that was that.

Anyway, we had had the fun of catching the eel, so we nudged it back into the water and watched it go. But we still weren't done with it. Later that morning we took the boat down to the other end of the lake, where there was a little store plus a dozen small cottages. "How's the fishing?" asked somebody at the store.

Dad, with the fisherman's usual talkativeness, merely grunted that it was "okay," in spite of a number of fine catches we'd enjoyed. But I was too full of the wonder of eels to let it go at that. "Gosh," I blurted, "you should have seen the eel we got!"

I went on to describe our prize—how it thrashed all over the place and tied itself in knots. I told how it was yellow and black in the water. Doubtless I warmed up as I went along, and was just about to give the story its glorious out-of-the-tub climax when the store owner cut me short.

"Sonny," he said quickly, "how about a lift with these boxes? Right out into the back yard, okay?" His request was so unusual and his tone so urgent that I picked up the boxes and followed him. But when we were out of the store his manner changed.

"Listen," he said, in a tone that would have done credit to a purveyor of French postcards, "let me tell you something. I've got every one of my cabins full. People go swimming at our beach all day long. Now, I can't let them know there's eels in the lake, can I? Why, they'd be scared to death to go into the water!"

I stared at him. Before I could think of a suitable answer, he finished his little course in public relations. "You see," he confided, "not everybody's the same way. Just because you—uh, we—like eels is no sign *everybody* likes 'em. So the less we say the better. Right?"

It was almost my first inkling that there were creatures on this earth that people might shy away from. And the store-keeper was in earnest, too. He even gave me a candy bar as hush money. I mumbled a lame excuse when someone asked me further about the eel, and fled to the safety of our boat.

I was embarrassed and contrite and in dread that my ill-timed recital would precipitate a general exodus from all twelve cabins. I ate the candy on the way home, but only out of a sense of duty. And it was with immense relief that I noted the cabins were still occupied the following day.

After that little experience I tried to keep my enthusiasm to myself—especially with animals that seemed to conjure mixed emotions in people. With regard to eels, I guess the trouble is that most persons see all that wiggle and think of some sort of waterborne reptile—an undersized sea monster at worst, or a snake at best. Then, too, the thought of an eel brings to mind a scissor-jawed moray in a tropical lagoon somewhere. There it lurks, ready to divest you of an arm or leg when you come blundering along with your mask and flippers.

Actually, eels aren't quite that way. Not even morays, which are not true eels at all, but elongated fish in a group

171

all their own. The little pet turtle in your aquarium is more closely related to a snake, or to some reptilian sea monster, than an eel could ever be.

An eel is nothing but a fish. It has gills like a fish and fins like a fish, even though these fins are reduced to a single pair near the head. It also has an undulating fringe which runs clear around the tail from back to belly—a combined dorsal, ventral and caudal fin. Its tiny scales are so reduced as to be microscopic; their protective function is partially assumed by glands secreting that much-criticized slime—a substance of many uses.

So in truth *Anguilla rostrata* (scientifically, "the long, slender body with a snout at the tip") is really a distant cousin of the active little guppies or the placid goldfish in your aquarium. To me it is one of the most graceful creatures on this earth. But I still remember that storekeeper—in whose mind, unhappily, the eel finds himself in company with the animals nobody loves.

Well, almost nobody. Go to a fancy food store and you'll find pieces of smoked eel, cut across the grain so they resemble small-caliber chunks of liverwurst. Parceled out in little bits, an eel is much more acceptable. Just *how* acceptable you can tell by a look at the astonishing price tags they bear. Or, for the European touch, find a market that sells elvers, civelles or anguilas—English, French and Spanish for "baby eels," respectively. They will be preserved in glass like caviar, tinned like sardines, dried like prunes or swimming in wine. And again, note the price tag.

But these are all safely bottled and smoked and marinated. Live eels, gliding through the water or creating a ruckus at the end of your fishline, are something else again. As a neighbor of mine recalled when I asked her if, in all her years of dedicated fishing, she had ever caught an eel in Lake Champlain:

"Catch an eel? I should say I did. My father cut the line for me so the thing could get away. And I've worried for twenty years for fear I'd catch another one!"

You take the shape, add the squirm, and cover it all with a viscous coating and there's probably plenty of reason for people to consider twice before hauling an eel ashore. But, just as with any other living thing you could name, its looks are really an outward sign of a marvelous adaptation to its life. Everything about an eel—like everything about an eagle or an ermine or an elephant—fits perfectly.

It *has* to fit. The eel walks an ecological tightrope just as much as a tortoise or a mouse or a robin. Tip the balance just a bit and the animal dies. The crucial point may be food or camouflage; it may be the ability to hide its eggs, or just the capacity to stay in one place. Eels constantly have to keep from being eaten; at the same time they have to satisfy their own prodigious appetites.

If you want to see one of these tightropes, walk along a rocky coast. The boulders around you are covered with snails. A certain species thrives only at high-tide line. Another lives at extreme low, with still others at several definite levels in between. Your steps, no matter how careful, dislodge a whelk here, a periwinkle there. Some of the unfortunate creatures roll on the rocks to the wrong zone. Others are merely over-turned. But each has been thrust into perils from which it may never recover.

Just the fact that it is upside down may be fatal. The little mollusc will have to stretch that soft body out to turn over again. For a snail, it rights itself quickly; it has to. But the eyes of gulls and sandpipers are sharp.

Spotting that white undersurface of the shell lying un-naturally against the darker rock, the birds keep a close watch, waiting to nip the creature when it ventures to turn itself over. If it waits for the return of the tide, it may be found by the ever-active rock crabs. A quick pinch disables the snail—and then it's only a matter of time.

Right side up and fully at home, the snail "belongs" perfectly. In the same manner, an eel fits its own spot in life. Its slender shape, strong snout and protruding lower jaw allow it to muscle its way through the mud and weeds. It overturns stones and pokes around in the debris. An eel samples everything in its path—molluscs, crayfish, worms, little fish, edible plant material, even carrion. It is like an animated vacuum cleaner.

The eel generally stays buried in the mud in the daytime. Its olive-gray back and sides match its surroundings. Its yellow underside resembles the muddy water against the sky to any enemy peering up from below.

And eels have plenty of enemies. Almost any fisherman knows this. Bass like them; so do pike and perch, among others. You can buy small eels, gazing at you from within a jar of brine, at any bait store worth its name. You can even buy empty eelskins. These you fix up with a weight and a few hooks—and you've got a sure-fire rig for salt-water bluefish. Ospreys and terns drop down from the sky on big and little eels. Snapping turtles prowl through the mud and lunge at anything that moves; the slime of an eel is of no avail in the four-edged vise of the snapper's mouth. The slime doesn't help the eel that falls into the clutches of an otter or mink, either.

Granted a thousand lucky escapes and a hundred thousand short-order meals, an eel may live for ten or a dozen years, unsuspected, in almost any pond. Eels have been found more than a mile high in mountain lakes. They have been found in rivers and brooks, all the way from their headwaters to the sea. They even mysteriously appear in landlocked farm ponds with no outlet. In captivity they're as hardy as a rich uncle, living as much as fifty years.

Russ W. Buzzell.

Were this all, the life of an eel would be as drab as the mud where it lives. But late some summer this begins to change. From this point to the end of its days the eel becomes the hero of one of the longest wedding marches on record. Actually, I should use the right term and say that it is a heroine. At least this is the case with the eels you catch in Lost Lake in Maine, say, or High Point Pond in the Smokies, or some similar spot remote from the sea. Almost every one of them is a female.

The males seldom go far inland. They spend their eight or ten years of bachelorhood on the coast, or at best in the mouth of a river. Half the size of their landlocked sisters, they are perhaps sixteen inches long when full grown. Their appetite is just as good, however, and they enter eelpots and fish weirs by the thousands as they putter around in search of food in the shallows. Like the females, it turns out that they are just marking time for the drama to come.

The coming excitement makes itself known in a way we human beings would recognize at once: the eels lose their appetites. Instead of scooping up almost anything and everything, they just cease to eat. All along their range—from Nova Scotia to the Gulf Coast—they swim unheedingly past the liveliest worms, the tastiest clams, the most seductive carrion. The same is true of the females in those faraway lakes. They all have, you might say, bigger fish to fry.

Now begins an urgent call. It is an old, old summons—some biologists say more than fifty million years old. And the eight-year-old males join the slightly older females in answering, as they have for eons. It is the call to the sea.

Not merely to the salt water, of course. The males are already there. But in comparison to the journey ahead they have yet to begin. They mill around as if awaiting further instructions. The activity of the females takes a more definite course. They start to make their way downstream.

176

EEL

If the lake empties into a river, the journey is easy. The females just follow the current. They drift along at night and burrow in the mud during the day. They don't eat a thing, even if the trip takes weeks and covers hundreds of miles. They have put on layers of fat; some of it is incorporated right into their flesh, and now this reserve is put to work. They go downstream by the dozens, scores, hundreds.

Often they come to a barrier. It may be a dam across the river, or merely a log which has fallen into the stream. Here is where the slimy body comes in. Waiting for a damp, dark night, the female creeps out of the water. Her slippery skin with its minute unseen scales lets her wriggle easily through the wet grass. She follows a hidden compass—the downward slope of the land, perhaps, or the dim light of the cloudy sky. Most likely she can sense the drift of trickling runoff if it has been raining.

The slime helps her in another way. It keeps her skin moist and pliable. The good supply of blood vessels lets the skin "breathe" a bit by absorbing a little oxygen from the air. If daylight comes and the eel is still out of water, she may find a damp spot to tide her over until night. Bedding down in the moist soil, she curls up and gulps air to stay alive. She may actually last through the day—a fish out of water.

Finally back in the stream, she swims with the current. In the fullness of time, she emerges into the saltiness of the sea.

Here the slime comes to her rescue again. To take just any freshwater fish and put it in the ocean is nearly always fatal. But the slippery coating serves as a buffer. Take an eel that has just gained the ocean's edge, wipe off the slime with a rough cloth, and put the eel back in the sea. Within a short time it dies in the unaccustomed saltiness. The reverse happens to a lobster put in fresh water; its delicate internal organs, taking in the strange new liquid, cannot long survive the change.

Thus protected by its gooey overcoat, the eel swims around as if it has lived in salt water all its life. Gradually it becomes attuned to its new habitat, finally adjusting perfectly.

As befits the occasion, the muddy-colored creature has put on a special attire. The eel is now almost black, with a bronze side and a snowy belly—the delicate-flavored "silver eel." Exclusive food stores honor its new status with exclusive price tags. As plain old "yellow eel" it had cost only half as much.

Now begins the mystery. No sooner have the females materialized in the sea and joined the males than they both disappear. I have seen pairs of eels idly nosing among the shallows at Rocky Neck State Park on the Connecticut coast, but they may well have been two males of differing sizes, still in their adolescence. On the other hand, they just might have been some of these pubescent eels, as they're called, pairing up for the long journey ahead. The truth is that nobody knows yet whether they travel in pairs or singly, in stag lines or hen parties.

The destination of our common American eel is in the same general area sought by its European cousin—a thousand miles away in the deep waters off Bermuda. Or at least that's what all the evidence indicates. The first eel has yet to be seen swimming en route there. The common creature that thrilled me—and placed the Maine storekeeper in a dilemma—just drops out of sight.

Does it go along with its fellows in a tenuous skein of eels undulating over the bottom? Many biologists think so. On the other hand, perhaps it pursues its course all by itself without regard to others of its kind. Nobody is sure how it travels. Once it has left the shelter of the bays and coasts, the eel will never be seen by man again. An occasional sick individual may drift ashore or blunder into a deep-sea trawl, but such cases are so rare that they give us hardly any clues. In these

178

oceanic specimens the eyes have enlarged tremendously, probably for better vision in the murky depths.

There is a huge clockwise whirlpool in the ocean off the eastern coast of North America. It is caused by the sun's heat and the turning of the earth, and occupies much of the broad Atlantic between the New World and the Old. The warm waters of the Gulf Stream enter it at about four miles per hour, and slow down as they split off easterly toward Europe. A spot near the center of this slow maelstrom is the destination of the eels. They will meet in the depths beneath a floating mass of weeds known as the Sargasso Sea.

Giving the eels their usual swimming speed of about half a mile per hour for twelve or thirteen miles a day, they should arrive at the Sargasso Sea in late winter. Some eels have to go twice as far as others, so the arrivals may be spread over weeks. During the eels' migration their reproductive structures have developed. The occasional captured specimen shows huge masses of eggs or long ribbonlike spermatic organs.

All this activity—the perilous trip downstream, the long journey to the Sargasso Sea, and the enormous development of the sex organs—takes place without a bite of food. The stomachs of those few eels that have been captured are always empty; their intestines have withered away.

Spawning apparently takes place down there in the blackness and pressure. Perhaps the day will come when we can witness the mating act. Now, however, we can only guess. Some of the other three-hundred-odd species of eels reproduce in far shallower water, and we have been able to pry into their affairs. From their activity we can deduce what must go on among this American eel species some thousand feet below that great floating mat of sargassum weed.

The male may press against the female, winding partially around her and forcing the eggs from her by his embrace. At

179

the same time the "milt," or sperm, is emitted. With millions of eels possibly mating at the same time, there must be a tumult of egg and sperm and writhing bodies down there in the dark. Nobody knows if one male fertilizes only a single female or if the future generation represents the general aftermath of one big family reunion.

And quite an aftermath it is. Each female may produce as many as five million eggs. Thus she is one of the most prolific creatures in a group where big families are commonplace. Every egg is endowed with a speck of yolk and a tiny droplet of oil. The oil, being less dense than water, causes the egg to float. It drifts away from the unheeding parents, a tiny grain of tapioca in the boundless bowl that is the sea.

This is probably the final effort of the parents. It has been a long struggle without food, and now, most likely, the adults sink, dying, into the three-mile abyss below them. But in truth we just don't know. Not a single "spent" eel has ever been recovered.

The main story, of course, goes on. The babies that hatch from those floating eggs look more like flounders than eels. Flattened from side to side, each one is oblong, like a tiny leaf. A feeble fin around the rear of the body is barely enough to move it about in the water. It drifts, with the billions of its brothers and sisters and cousins, slowly carried by ocean currents.

Like any baby it has a strong hold on life. Just the incredible numbers of these leptocephalus larvae (literally, "the strap with a head") is fine group life insurance.

And food is close at hand, too: each larva can snap up tiny plankton organisms floating right along with it. Another point in its favor is that the larva is almost completely transparent. You could lay it on the page of this book and read the print through it.

The only way you are likely to discover a leptocephalus in

180

the ocean is to note its eyes. These twin black dots drift along seemingly in disembodied pairs through the warm waters. Even under the microscope the tiny innards are barely visible, with a ghostly heart pumping the thinnest traces of blood among them. Instead of a backbone there is a rod of cartilage, the notochord, supporting the fragile body.

These self-reliant bits of nothing take a year to grow. Even then they're scarcely impressive, being still transparent and barely three inches long. Now, able to guide their course a bit, they veer off at a tangent or ride those currents that will bring them close to the shores from which their parents came.

It is easy to dismiss a year in a paragraph, but that's about all one can do, for these youngsters are still shrouded in mystery. However, they must face a withering crossfire of enemies. Other fish, squid, crustaceans, and even jellyfish doubtless take a terrific toll. Nobody seems to have determined their survival rate; one in ten thousand, perhaps, or one in a hundred thousand. Amid all the uncertainties of their perilous lives, one thing is sure: most of them probably never make it.

The thousand-mile trip of the American eel would be just a short jaunt for its cousin from the east side of the Atlantic. The European eel travels three or four times that distance to the same general area in the Sargasso Sea. When the American species puts to shore, the European eel still has two years to go. It floats a full three years before it approaches the coast of England, Spain, Denmark. Thus the European eel has one of the longest babyhoods of any fish in existence.

At the end of one or three years, depending on the species, the next stage unfolds. Daily the leptocephalus changes its shape. The flattened body becomes more slender. The notochord is replaced by a chain of vertebrae. In a few weeks, cradled in the sea water, the leptocephalus has become an eel.

Still almost transparent, the fingerling "glass eel" wriggles its way through the water with the swarms of its companions.

As their legions gain the mouths of the rivers and work up toward the fresh water, the eels begin to lose their invisibility. Gradually pigment is laid down in the tissues until they are readily apparent to the naked eye; now they become elvers, those slender creatures with the interesting name that you may have met at some gourmet restaurant. In the absence of any tagging data it is still a question whether or not they enter the same river their parents knew.

During the day most of the elvers stay hidden in the mud. At night, however, they move steadily upstream in a long, silent, apparently endless procession. So powerful is their urge to penetrate fresh water that, if bottles of fresh water are un-stopped in a tank of sea water containing elvers, they all will obediently enter the bottles. The coming of these tasty morsels in England brings about an "eel fair," where nets, buckets and even bare hands are used to scoop them out of the water.

I saw a procession of elvers last April along the Virginia shore. A small brackish stream, so narrow you could easily step over it, ran from a large swampy area. The stream tumbled over a single log that had been placed across it as a dam. The elvers assembled below this wooden barrier just at dusk and swam around like animated gray lollipop sticks. They were arriving, singly and in small groups, from the ocean three miles away.

Peg and I watched the elvers for several minutes. There were perhaps two hundred of them at the foot of the little dam. Then my wife went back to the car to look for a scoop. The only thing she found was a paper bag. Dipping it into the water, she captured several dozen of the active creatures. Hastily, before the bag broke, she released them above the dam. They twisted and wriggled in what we assured ourselves was gratitude. Then they pointed those slender bodies upstream and disappeared into the shadows.

Although the wooden dam was an inconvenience to the elvers, it was no barrier. After a gantlet which had lasted a year and stretched a thousand miles, they could hardly be turned back by a water-soaked log. Indeed, at one corner where stringy soil provided a little footing, several of them were climbing up on the damp surface. We watched as they fell back again and again. Occasionally one would be successful, and, its latest hurdle conquered, would swim off unconcernedly upstream.

Many brooks drained that brackish swamp. Each of them probably held its share of eels. Multiply the two hundred elvers we saw on that single evening by the thousands of streams and rivers on the Atlantic coast, and carry this over a number of nights for perhaps a month. Then remember that these represent only the remnant of a far larger population. It is not hard to understand why some biologists feel that the American eel and its look-alike European cousin constitute the most numerous vertebrate animals alive.

One railroad station in France shipped more than seventy tons of elvers for food during a single season. This represented over one hundred million individuals. Doubtless the fishermen who caught them would say you should have seen the little ones that got away.

Eels apparently have their own idea as to where to settle down. A large percentage of males and a goodly sprinkling of females merely poke around the bottom muck of a shallow coastal bay for the rest of their adolescent lives; a few other males go a bit farther. The bulk of the journey is left to the females, however, and they push upstream against all odds. I have seen eels working their way up along the crevice of a rock behind a waterfall. Other times they're content to swim around for several years in the pool at the base of the cataract. So valued are eels to the European taste that long, inclined culverts or "eel tubes" are sometimes installed to get them around giant dams, like the fish ladders on this side of the Atlantic.

Finally, swimming along and crawling on wet nights, the eel finds just the spot. There it takes up residence for eight or ten years, feeding all summer and drowsing in the mud during the winter. Its voracious appetite turns the tables, in a way, on the finny world that made its life so hazardous in days gone by. And its willingness to try anything once results in a flabbergasted farm boy who suddenly finds an eel on the end of his line down at the pasture pond.

Once settled in its chosen home, the eel may stay for six or eight years. It finds its living within a few hundred feet of some central resting place until it is called back to the sea.

Lacking the truth about eels, the ancients made up their own tales. Feared and therefore hated, they have been guessed about, lied about, cussed and discussed ever since man began to tell fish stories. No less an authority than Aristotle declared that they came full-formed from the mud. An old book on natural history elaborated on his theory. "They develop from the humours and vapours of the darkest swamps," it intoned, "and are every bit as vile." Early fishermen, capturing an eel in their nets, often dumped the entire haul back overboard; the creature's slime supposedly poisoned the whole catch.

For a long time the eel was thought to be sexless. "It begets its young by rubbing against stones and other objects, shredding its skin," solemnly vowed a seventeenth-century authority. "These pieces of flesh then swim off to become new eels." In this, the author was quoting Pliny's ancient *Natural History*, back two thousand or so years ago when such intriguing things caused little wonder.

Actually, the confusion was only natural. All the eels examined in fresh water look the same internally. They are, for

184

the most part, virgin females whose sex organs have not begun to develop. None of them contains eggs. The males in the bays are scarcely different; they haven't matured either. Only after the eels are on their way to the Sargasso Sea does development of sex organs take place.

To confuse matters further, those little leaflike larvae hardly look like eels. Up until the last century they were thought to be a distinct species. All that was known, really, was that large eels disappear into the sea in the fall and slender elvers appear in the rivers in spring.

It remained for a Danish fisheries expert, Johannes Schmidt, to put the pieces of the puzzle together. Working for twenty years, patiently drawing his nets and asking questions of hundreds of fishermen, he followed the largest leptocephalus larvae progressively on their back trail. Smaller and smaller larvae came to light in the drifting currents. Then in 1922, Schmidt and his assistants found the smallest, tiny and quite obviously just hatched, in the Sargasso Sea. The mysterious birthplace of the eels had been discovered.

There is one thing more—in a way the most exciting of all. The youthful stages of a plant or animal give some hints about their ancestry. For instance, human beings show a striking similarity in our embryonic development to a fish. We even have gill slits at one stage of our growth; at another point we have a tail; and at still another we resemble all unborn mammals, from mouse to pig to whale—in such a degree that the common ancestry of all seems inescapable. In the annual spring convocation of frogs and toads in the swamps for egg-laying, scientists feel that the goggle-eyed creatures are hearkening back to forgotten aquatic ancestors. This belief is borne out further by the fishy, wiggly tadpoles that appear a couple of weeks later.

So the eel, conceived in the pressure and blackness of the ocean depths, spends a few years on shore, as it were. Then, having favored us landlubbers with its presence, it returns to the deeps from which it came. In so doing, it may be retracing a venerable path, finding its way back through eons to its ancestral home, like a living fossil.

Australian, African and Asiatic eels have the same general life story. But with deep water almost at hand off their coasts, the journey is less spectacular. They have no continental shelf to swim over to reach the necessary depths. And the eels that spend their entire lives in the ocean have little need to travel. They are already at home in the sea water, anyway. Some scientists feel they represent an early type that is apparently content to remain in its primeval home.

Among the three hundred other species of fish honored by designation as eels, there are a number of creatures that are as oddball in their habits as they are in their looks. There is the electric eel, for instance, which lives in South American rivers. It can deliver a wallop of three hundred volts or more—enough to stun a horse. It uses its power for defense or for shocking small food fish.

One of the largest varieties is the conger eel of our Atlantic shallows. It has been known to reach more than eight feet in length and fifty pounds in weight. One, reeled right to the top of the fishpole by an excited fisherman, threw a loop around the pole and bent it double. Faced with such antics, the fisherman threw the whole works into the water.

One eel lives in the sand of shallow waters. It makes its way into its chosen domain by vibrating its tail rapidly, working backward down in the ocean floor like an animated jackhammer. From here it makes periodic forays for food. Another eel lives between the half-opened shells of giant clams. It ventures forth for food, beating a hasty retreat to the shelter of its massive host when some larger fish goes after it.

Occasionally the great shells snap shut on the eel's pur-

186

suer and the little opportunist proceeds to dine on the lifeless body of his would-be captor. Although he is wonderfully agile, the eel himself may occasionally be caught by his gigantic landlord.

Or take the case of the parasitic snub-nosed eel of half a mile down. Apparently it needs surroundings with more personality than is afforded by a stolid clam the size of a washtub. The little eel finds a suitable large fish. Then it nips its way in through the body wall of its intended host. It spends its growing years in its living surroundings, feeding on the tissues of its unwilling cafeteria. Apparently, like a well-adjusted tapeworm, it takes only enough of nonvital tissues for its own needs. Thus it won't eat itself out of house and home.

The snub-nosed eel's methods may remind you of the lamprey "eel"—which, incidentally, is not an eel at all. It is not even a fish, but a special creature in a group of its own. It is known scientifically as a cyclostome (literally, "circular mouth"), and belongs to a group of primitive vertebrates whose ancestors predated the fishes. Lampreys are weak-eyed or blind, with just a tail fin, and a skeleton composed of cartilage. Wriggling through the water until it comes to some large moving object, the lamprey clings with a suckerlike mouth. If the object is a fish, the lamprey rasps a meal from the soft body with its sharp teeth.

If the object is a boat or turtle, the lamprey merely hitches a ride. Such freeloaders accompanied ships through canals from the sea and nearly ruined the Great Lakes fishing industry. Today scientists are able to treat the spawning brooks with a larvicide relatively harmless to other life but lethal to young lampreys. They can also erect stream barriers that can be leaped by trout but not baby lampreys. Electrical traps in the water prevent the adults from ascending these brooks to lay their eggs. So the lamprey is getting his comeuppance.

187

But, in the meantime, this "eel" that isn't an eel gives a bad name to the eel that is. And the true eel, Heaven knows, needs all the friends he can get.

Even the moray "eel" is a victim of a whispering campaign. Like many another creature seen from a strictly human viewpoint, his looks are against him. That gaping mouth and the head poking out of an undersea cavern are scarcely calculated to inspire confidence. And the moray—from the little specimen scarcely two feet long to great striped or spotted or green individuals that may exceed six feet—is capable of living up to his reputation.

Yet like most other creatures, including man himself, his main desire is just to be let alone. Those wire-cutter jaws—with or without the added refinement of a few sharp teeth—are meant for seizing unwary fish. If you carelessly reach into a moray's retreat, your hand may resemble an unwary fish, too. But, as a friend of mine who goes scuba-diving in the Bahamas observed, "Heck, they don't bother you if you don't bother them. I swim right past them all the time. But if you go after a moray with a spear gun, chances are he'll argue the point with you right there."

Morays have their own troubles. That expanse of smooth skin, hidden quietly much of the time in an undersea crevice, collects its share of little fellow-travelers. These may be marine worms, fish lice and other small crustaceans. Their unwanted attentions must make life uncomfortable for the moray. Finally he is stirred up enough to do something about them.

Hauling his length out of his den, the moray hies himself to a nearby coral garden. There, waving their long antennae as they sense his approach, a number of delicate shrimp await their visitor. The moray settles down among them. He patiently bides his time while they go over him like little garbage collectors. Although he could snap the shrimp up in a trice, he

188

quietly allows them to depopulate his exterior. They even reach those slender pincers down into his mouth to extract bits of food. It must feel good to have such a thorough massage.

Finally cleanup time is over. The little shrimp waft away from the moray on tiptoe like multicolored ballet dancers. Rousing himself, their well-scoured host goes back to his lair minus his star boarders—and once again becomes the fearsome monster of the reefs.

This is only partly the story of the eel. And, as with almost any living creature, the facts are as strange as the fabrications. You can't help but feel a twinge of compassion for the moray that has an itch and nothing to scratch it with. You've got to admire the steadfastness of the American and European eels, finding their way from some remote pond to the depths of the Sargasso Sea. And then there is the incredible odyssey of the delicate babies over thousands of miles to the same or similar ponds a year or two later.

It so staggers the imagination that even the most implacable eel-hater must give them credit for perseverance. It's the very least we can do for a critter which for centuries was supposed to rub against underwater objects to shred off a few babies now and then.

Coyote

THE match burned my hand. I shook it out and waited, listening. Peg straightened up from setting the picnic table. Our four children, silhouetted against the sunset on top of the little mesa, stood still as statues.

The sound came again. A series of short yip-yips, followed by a long, quavering howl. It was answered by another wail, more distant than the first. Then by another, so loud that it seemed only beyond the next little hill.

There was a rattle of pebbles from the children on the mesa. Then a clatter, as four small bodies tumbled down amidst the

rubble and raced for the shelter of the camp. They stood
there, wide-eyed. A delicious tingle ran through all of us as
the ghostly chorus rose and fell.

Our eldest daughter spoke what was on all our minds.
"Coyotes!" said Janice. "Real, live coyotes!"

That ghostly serenade wrapped the day up perfectly for
the family of a naturalist. As campers and travelers we already
enjoy the outdoors; with our added interest in plants and
animals we savor each trip to the full. Every gasoline stop,
every turnoff at a rest area is likely to become an event. And
a three-part oratorio by the little prairie wolf was an unexpected bonus.

We had traveled through some of the most unfairly named
scenery on the face of this continent—the starkly beautiful Bad-
lands—and had finally stopped for the night at a tiny campground. There were eight picnic tables, with trailers at seven
of them. The remaining site had a smooth sandy area; in fifteen minutes our little tent had blossomed in the middle of it.

Fifteen minutes later the coyotes had begun their serenade.
And in fifteen more minutes two campsites were vacant.
Their occupants had hastily closed their trailers, flung themselves into their cars, and driven off into the gloom. Doubtless
they spent the night putting as many miles as possible between
them and those ravenous beasts—unless they managed to find
a motel somewhere.

As Peg and I snugged the tent ropes to the picnic table
against the steady push of the prairie wind, the man from the
next campsite strolled over. "Well," he observed, looking
after the escaping tourists, "they sure lit out of here in a
hurry."

"Yep," I agreed. "They sure did. Guess they'd never heard
a coyote before."

"Frankly, neither have I." He watched us for a moment.
"Say, the wife's got some iced tea over in the trailer. And

maybe we can find a soda for the kids. Come on over when you get a minute."

That's the way it is with campers. We have found them to be some of the friendliest people we could ever meet. Complete strangers invite you in for a snack; if you're having trouble they'll volunteer their services. So, after we'd finished supper we took them up on their offer.

We talked more than an hour with the gentleman and his wife. They apparently had invited the whole campground, too, for there were about ten of us sitting around their picnic table. Our conversation pivoted around that chorus at sunset —how coyotes had howled just beyond the campfire for centuries. We sat around the light of a gasoline lantern and recalled all the coyote stories we could think of. None of them lost anything in the telling, either.

Finally the time came to break up. Our host was reluctant to see us go. Peg and I headed for the tent. "Need a flashlight?" my friend asked.

"Heck, no," Tom answered for us. "We're just over there."

"I guess you're right," our new acquaintance said. But he still shone a light for us as we made our way back home. Only after I found our own light and began to shine it around the tent's canvas interior did I hear him enter the door of his trailer.

Now, as I look back on it, I should have known at once the reason for all his interest in our welfare. But in a moment it became clear, anyway. Scarcely had I retired before Peg called me to get up again. Last to turn in, she had just been picking her way across the quiet forms of her offspring when she had happened to glance out the entrance of the tent. Now she directed my attention to that trailer.

The man and his wife had just come down the steps of their little two-wheeled home. After sweeping the beam of the flashlight under the trailer and the car, they went out by the corner of their campsite. Then slowly, carefully, they scanned every inch of the Dakota landscape with that light—including a surreptitious look at the area around our tent.

Apparently satisfied, they went back into the trailer. In a few minutes we heard a stealthy sound: the click-squeak of the trailer windows being halfway closed.

And so, having guarded themselves and these defenseless tenters from Vermont against the terrible coyotes Out There Somewhere, they retired to the steamy protection of the trailer.

We hoped to hear the coyotes again at sunrise, but that single recital was all they were going to allow us. I expressed my disappointment when our new friends emerged the next morning.

Considering the uneasiness with which they had committed themselves to the hazards of a night on the Dakota plains, their reply was surprising.

"We're sorry we couldn't hear them again, either," the woman said. "But at least we had that howling last night. They'll never take that away from us. Never."

Her husband nodded. "We've been on the road more than a month, now. And that's the most wonderful thing that's happened yet. It was kind of scary, I must admit. But if we don't see or hear another thing, it'll make the whole trip worth while."

They were from Baltimore, it turned out, and were on their way to visit their son in Oregon. As I considered the thrill with which they'd tell of the time they were surrounded by coyotes in South Dakota, I realized that *el coyote*—the clever one—was perhaps making himself a new name. Except for campers who take off down the road in terror, the reaction to his howl out there in the dark may be one of delighted fascination. Perhaps even of anticipation, as flashlights sweep through the gloom from the safety of a trailer. He might actually become a valued tourist attraction.

But this will take awhile. At present, he has a lot to live down. Some of this is of his own doing, it is true. Much of it, however, is just because the rangy, tireless thirty-pounder is so talented that he *could* have done all those heinous things ascribed to him, even if he *didn't*. So therefore he's guilty, or he ought to be.

The first mistake of the prairie wolf—to use that name by which he is often known on the Plains—was just in being there. He got along fine with the North American Indian; in fact, Indian legends are full of tales of the wisdom and cleverness of the coyote. But when the white man came and claimed the New World for his own, anything that stood in the way of Progress had to be eliminated.

There are few cases where a human hand has been laid more heavily on a wild creature. Many birds and animals, under far less persecution than the coyote, have vanished entirely. The passenger pigeon, the Carolina parakeet, the great auk, Steller's sea cow and the dodo will never be seen alive again. None of these was the subject of an entire three centuries of hate—and dogs, and guns, and traps and poison. None was hunted with the avowed purpose of erasing its very name from the face of the earth. Yet all have passed away. Even as that last forlorn passenger pigeon took her final breath in the St. Louis Zoo in 1914, some of the very human beings who read of her death were plotting new ways to bring about the same fate for the coyote and his larger cousin, the timber wolf.

The timber wolf indeed seems headed down the trail to extinction. The coyote, however, is more fortunate. It appears to thrive on everything man has thrown at it. It is one of the few predatory animals on the face of our earth that is actually extending its range.

The coyote's cleverness is what has led to its survival. This is what infuriates man: the critter is so confounded smart.

COYOTE

It matters not, of course, that the coyote was there first, getting along in perfect harmony with the jackrabbits and prairie dogs and kangaroo rats. Nor does it matter that the Great Plains bore fabulous numbers of wildlife when European man first arrived. As quail and grouse and pronghorn became scarcer, a scapegoat had to be found. So man looked beyond his plows and his eroded soil and his grass fires and his devouring herds—and saw a coyote standing against the sky.

Having decided on the culprit, man has sought to run him off the land. After all, that's what "scapegoat" is supposed to mean literally—a goat you saddle with your problems and allow to escape, taking your woes with him. But the coyote has refused to play the part. In fact, with maddening aplomb, the outcast has cheerfully turned into an opportunist. He even has won a few allies among the very persons who were supposed to do him in.

To explain this perverse turn of affairs, it will help to pry into the coyote's home life. As if in regard for the human calendar—or, perhaps, with complete disdain for it—the round of coyote life can be said to begin neatly in January. It comes full circle just a year later.

Coyotes are normally indifferent to any long-lasting social ties. They may call in unison from separate hilltops at dusk or dawn, but this is apparently for little more than the music of it all. After the chorus has ceased they go their various ways—or, at most, in twos and threes. These little groups may be merely a mother and a couple of cubs reluctant to let go of the apron strings, or they may be a pair of coyotes temporarily allied for the purpose of hunting.

In January, however, things begin to look different. The little female who has been so adept at stalking jackrabbits all year—creeping forward while they're feeding, standing stock-

still when they look up—becomes careless about her range boundaries. Instead of wandering perhaps five miles at a time, she goes eight or ten. This, just by chance, leads her to the territory of that forty-pound baritone over by the dry stream-bed.

He, in his turn, may be off on some errand of his own. Her wanderings thus accomplish little more than a change of scenery. However, since coyotes are really wild dogs, each deposits a few routine drops of urine at scent posts along the way. Then, on the next trip around, a long and sober sniffing —plus a new addition to the bulletin board—begins to make things interesting. And sooner or later boy meets girl.

It is at this stage that animal taxonomists—classification experts—sometimes find their troubles beginning. The coyote is much like a small, light-colored German shepherd in appearance, but with a bushier tail. It holds the tail low in running, not high as does a dog or wolf. Actually, though, it is not in superficial looks that the trouble occurs; it's in the ease with which family lines are breached. *Canis latrans*, the coyote (literally, "barking dog"), may, in her wandering, come face to face with *Canis familiaris* (the "familiar dog," or if you prefer, Rover or Blaze). Normally, she would turn tail and streak it for the high country; and hot on her heels would come Blaze with blood in his eye.

Female coyotes have periodic times of heat, just like their domestic counterparts. If a female in breeding condition meets a male dog, there probably will be a chase, but the end result may be different. Blaze misses a few meals and arrives back at the ranch dog-tired—after having bestowed his affection on his wild little playmate. Some nine weeks later, she presents the world with eight or ten Blaze-yotes—or, to use a term familiar to game managers, coy-dogs.

The trick can work the other way. An intrepid male coyote may happen on Lady or Susie when she's in heat. The alliance gives rise to a few half-and-half mementos of the occasion.

No matter which parent is which, the youngsters usually resemble both. They are likely to be larger than either, though, as is often the case with hybrids. Gifted with the native abilities of each species, but often not fully accepted by either, coy-dogs may become outcasts. They carve out a living as best they can. Large enough to track deer down in the snow —something their smaller coyote parents seldom do—they enlist the aid of a stray dog or two, and soon run afoul of man and his guns. My own Green Mountain state of Vermont has had coy-dogs for years; apparently they are the result of the steady eastward spread of the coyote from the Lake States through the Adirondacks.

If things go more normally, however, the male and female coyote begin to run together from that January day when they touch noses. Sometimes they remain together for the rest of the year, occasionally even for life. They are intensely loyal to each other. They hunt together, doze on a sunny hillside together, sing duets to the evening sun or the waning moon together.

They may even die together if one is so unfortunate as to become trapped. Its mate, refusing to abandon the captive to its fate, brings rabbits and ground squirrels as food. A hunter with whom I spoke in Wyoming says that a coyote will even soak in a stream and lie down next to its thirsty captive mate, who gratefully chews on the damp fur. Making use of such faithfulness, it is sometimes possible, if a "varmint" trapper is callous enough, to leave a trapped coyote as bait for its distraught mate.

Barring such a tragedy, the pair of coyotes makes an unbeatable hunting team. Capable of sprinting as fast as forty miles an hour for short stretches, with sustained runs of half that speed, the coyote can often catch a jackrabbit. But when hunting in pairs it may employ a whole bag of tricks and save the speed for real emergencies. Often one of the pair will hide while the other hunts. Then, when Coyote Number Two flushes a rabbit, the race will be maneuvered into a great circle. This brings the rabbit around to Number One, who then leaps, fresh and strong, into the chase while Two drops out.

One of the swiftest animals of the Plains is the pronghorn. This New World relative of the chamois, incorrectly called an antelope, can outrun a coyote on the straightaway. But the clever little predators usually wait until the pronghorn is at some disadvantage. Then they'll endeavor to run alongside it, one on either side, perhaps a hundred yards apart. The pronghorn veers back and forth between them, thus wasting valuable effort. Or, if the coyotes can get the pronghorn started running around a hill, one will continue in pursuit while the other takes a short cut over the top of the hill.

Then there's the old dodge, sometimes used by foxes as well, which might be called "what-you-can-see-can't-hurt-you." A coyote will go blundering down into a valley inhabited by several potential dinners. As he crashes along, he yips and yelps and makes a fine stir. Naturally, every rabbit or prairie dog in the vicinity runs for cover. Safely at the edge of a shelter, the small animals watch, fascinated, as the coyote puts on his display. Too late, of course, does some unlucky victim realize that there are really *two* coyotes: one brash and loud, the other stealthy and quiet, sneaking up from behind.

Aided and abetted by the equivalent of one prairie dog per day (or, now that prairie dogs have become scarce, an equal volume of ground squirrels, mice or jackrabbits) the coyotes make their way through the western two thirds of North America. Once given to running along a ridge so they could watch both sides, they eventually learned, somehow, that this put them in good silhouette for a man with a gun. Now they

200

run along what modern infantrymen call "the military crest" —a spot just short of the top but which still affords a good view. Or, as coyotes are quite strongly nocturnal, they may lie all day on a convenient sunny hillside. From this vantage point they watch the valley below for likely spots for the evening's hunting.

By mid-March the female feels the call to more domestic pursuits. She finds an abandoned badger hole, or the den of a marmot, or even a shelter in a jumble of rocks. She enlarges the hole until it has an entrance about a foot in diameter. Sometimes she brings in a few perfunctory wisps of grass or leaves. Often, however, she merely scoops out the interior of the burrow to make a cavern perhaps three feet in diameter and two feet high. This will be the nursery.

She may dig three or four such dens. When I learned that the females didn't settle on the first one built, I remarked to Peg that it was just like a woman—unable to make up her mind. Peg, however, said it was probably because a housewife never knows who is coming for dinner—in this case, coyote dinner. She was sure the surplus dens were for safety's sake, to confuse the enemy. And, apparently, my wife is right. The final den may have an extra exit or two as still another safety measure.

The pups are born sometime in April. Blind, helpless, with nondescript rough yellow-gray fur, they make up in numbers what they lack in looks. There may be up to a dozen of them, though six or seven is about average. Their mother stays right with them at first, going outside only for her personal needs. Her mate doubles his hunting efforts at the expense of hundreds of mice, ground squirrels and rabbits. Opportunist that he is, he is not above taking the eggs and young of ground-nesting birds as the season wears on. In fact, he readily pounces on almost anything that moves. He'll take fruit or berries in season, too.

Returning to the den with food for his mate, the male takes a devious route. Arriving in the vicinity, he may remain quietly hidden for an hour before making his way to the entrance. Or, if his ears and eyes and nose tell him all is clear, he runs directly home with the groceries—as one did in Montana, as if on cue, after I had been idly scanning a distant hillside with binoculars.

In about ten days the eyes of the pups begin to open. They are bleary-blue, as are the eyes of most juvenile mammals. The youngsters remain hidden, however, for about two weeks more. They become more active day by day, chewing on their patient mother one moment and on the ears of their littermates the next. They crawl and snuff their way around the little earthen cavern, recoiling from the unfamiliar light and air of the entrance.

At about four weeks their curiosity gets the best of them. Spilling out of the den, the tumbly little balls of fur come into the light for the first time. Any that are slow are carried to the entrance by their mother. For the next four weeks they behave in the rollicking manner of puppies the world over—pouncing on each other with grownup little growls, and stalking a beetle with nose to the ground and tail section high in the air.

By now it is late May or early June. Even without the constant danger of discovery by man, the pups have many enemies. Their parents cannot protect them all the time. With mother increasingly away from home, they face new hazards. Hawks and owls snatch them up with scarcely a pause in flight. Wildcats, cougars, even the badgers that dug the hole where they were born can make short work of them. The pups may be caught on any of the little trails they make from the den entrance to every nearby vantage point where they watch for their returning parents.

Three of the most effective enemies, though, have been

almost eliminated, thanks to man. These are the timber wolf, the wolverine and the golden eagle. Any of these large predators could make off with a pup right in the face of the parents. But now that the wolverine has been driven to the wilderness and the timber wolf is making his last stand, most coyotes will never even know of the existence of these great animals.

As for the golden eagle, its appearance almost anywhere is enough to bring out a dozen mighty hunters and their guns, apparently in an attempt to reassure themselves who's boss. The first living golden eagle I ever saw was brought to me, fatally wounded, by an ignoramus who shot it because, in his perverse logic, "any bird *that* big is up to no good, Ron."

With their enemies thinned out these days by man, a few of the pups have a good chance of making their way into full-scale coyotehood. Their parents teach them every step of the way. Ernest Thompson Seton wrote that coyotes have three means by which they can escape an early demise: instinct, their own experience, and the teachings of others of their kind. It is in this last department that the parent coyotes shine so eminently.

Catching a rabbit or ground squirrel, the parent carries it back to the den without killing it. Then it releases the prey for the pups. Now those mock attacks on windblown leaves and those stealthy caterpillar hunts are turned to the real thing. The unhappy recipient of all this attention makes off— sometimes to escape entirely—with half a dozen clumsy pups in eager pursuit.

Day after day this serious game is played. The cubs learn the characteristics of each animal—how the jackrabbit has wicked, flailing hind legs, how the spunky prairie dog can give a nasty cut with those buck teeth, and how the strong-armed gopher can dig himself into the soil as fast as the pups can dig him out.

They are weaned when they are about two months old. Soon they start out with their parents on nightly forays. With a warning growl their mother can send them scampering back behind her, just as she did at the den. Thus she teaches them the hazards of hornets and the perils of porcupines. She shows them the virtue of patience at the entrance of a marmot den and the value of snap judgment at the buzz of a rattlesnake. If she comes across something unwholesome or perilous—such as the traps or poisons of man—she may recoil as if shot. Or she may methodically bury it by flinging new earth over it.

The parents teach their youngsters a few short cuts, too. They demonstrate how to lie as if dead in the sun with those golden eyes almost shut—and then suddenly leap up and snap at a magpie or quail whose curiosity has brought it too close. They also show the youngsters that a wheeling, circling flock of ravens probably means food below. Since coyotes are not above carrion, this may mean the bonanza of a dead deer. By example, the youngsters learn to sit patiently, along with their parents, while a badger digs out a nest of wood rats. They wait in a circle, quickly snapping any hapless rodent that escapes the industrious digger.

They learn another thing too. Or, more properly, they practice what they already know, and that is to howl. Traditionally this takes place at the beginning and end of the coyote's day, and apparently has many meanings. It may be a call to hunt, an announcement of one's presence, a request for a communication from others, or merely a release of nervous energy.

Ernest Thompson Seton, describing the howl of the coyote, told how, when one began "the night song of the Plains," it was a signal for all, just as the fife and drum took hold of soldiers. And so with one coyote today: almost any moderately high-pitched noise will set it off. This may be the call of another coyote or the wail of a distant locomotive. Once it

204

has begun, the *yap-yap-yap-wo-o-o-o-w* may continue for half an hour, or even longer.

The loyalty of a mother to her cubs sometimes leads her to put her own life in grave danger. Although a coyote can easily escape a pack of dogs, a mother may find herself severely handicapped if caught away from home with her half-grown puppies. They run as fast and as far as they can until the little ones are so tired that they slow down. Then the mother, in a blaze of courage, may turn and run right back through the pack of dogs. This turns them away from the babies—but right on her heels with a tremendous advantage in favor of the dogs.

By August the cubs are able to take care of themselves. They often stay with their mother—and father, too, if his rather casual sense of domestic duty hasn't deserted him completely—until well into the fall. But a yen for independence finally sets them out on their own. They may hold a convocation from separate hilltops for the nightly serenade, but family ties have been severed.

In late December they are fully adult in everything but size. They may not attain maximum growth for two more years, and can expect to live perhaps ten years after that with extraordinary luck. But when January arrives, their small lives have come around to the beginning. It is mating time. With happy disregard for propriety, they seek whom they may of the opposite sex, and a new generation is on the way.

Such is the normal life of the coyote. There would seem to be little here to set man hard on his trail, breathing threatenings and slaughter. After all, what's so terrible about a critter that makes four-fifths of his living on mice, rabbits and ground squirrels—and tops them off with an occasional cleanup job on the carcass of a deer or bison?

The trouble, again, is that he is such a clever opportunist. And, remember, he was waiting when the first settlers came.

As those pioneers pushed onward, they brought with them their ducks and geese, pigs and cows, chickens and turkeys. These represented an unexpected windfall for Don Coyote: here was a whole banquet, just for the taking. It was easier to run down a squawking hen than to sneak up on her wild cousin, the prairie chicken. A cow was far more than he could tackle, even if he enlisted help, but a calf separated from its mother was pretty easy pickings.

He plunged joyfully into the melee. With the instinct of a million generations of forebears, and with the teachings of his parents still in his memory, he garnered every scrap. Doglike, he often buried the leftovers for future use. If he found himself in the midst of a flock of chickens, his almost automatic reflexes might keep him snapping at them until not a single one moved. An entire litter of pigs could not shelter under the capacious flanks of the sow; in fact, if the coyote worried her all night he might be able to get every last one. This was little more than the predatory urge in the face of such plenitude, somewhat like a child's rifling a box of chocolates; but the end result was as bad for the coyote's reputation as if the deed had been premeditated.

It didn't take long for the settlers to retaliate. Nor did it matter if the bonanza was all of man's own doing, spread out for the taking right in the lap of the coyote. The "varmint" had to go. Utterly and completely. He was nothing but a wolf, anyway, and everybody knew about wolves.

So the battle line was drawn. Only ten years after the Pilgrims landed, they set up a coyote and wolf bounty. The National Geographic Society says that in 1663, on Long Island, the person who killed a wolf was entitled to seven bushels of corn—after he had nailed the head to a suitable tree for all to admire.

And so it went. Colony after colony, territory after territory, and finally state after state put a price on the head of

206

"any wolf whatsoever." It mattered not whether the wolf or coyote had been caught in a particular act. Just the fact that it existed was proof of guilt.

The rewards were paid out in great shape. So brisk was the trade, and so lucrative, that bounties were quickly put on other creatures as well. If some critter ran afoul of your scheme—or threatened to—the bounty was supposed to solve everything. Porcupines, bobcats, skunks, weasels, seals, mountain lions, hawks and owls are among the many creatures which have enjoyed this token of man's esteem.

Until the 1950's America's national emblem, the bald eagle, was bountied in Alaska. Eagles were seen eating salmon just as they had done, probably, since the last ice age. It mattered not that most of the salmon was carrion, or at least dying adults who had spent their last energy in laying their eggs. The real culprit—commercial overfishing—continued on its gluttonous way, while the eagle was slaughtered in its innocence. Only in the last two decades has the great bird been given belated protection by our repentant forty-ninth state.

Even at this writing (fall 1970) the blot continues against "The Great Land," to use an Indian translation of the name of that wonderful far-northern state. Alaska has paid a wolf bounty since the last century. This is an attempt to eliminate the problem posed by the introduction of herds of semitame reindeer right on the home ground of the wolf. In 1921 the bounty was hiked from fifteen to a thumping fifty dollars per wolf, where it remains today. Hunted down from helicopters by brave men with high-powered rifles, each writhing wolf is a monument to shortsightedness. It is a strange way of doing things that permits the Alaskan variety of timber wolf to be driven to extinction even while the wolf as a species is placed on the United States Fish and Wildlife Service's endangered list.

So zealous are bounty-seekers that all manner of deeds

207

have been perpetrated to obtain the reward. Take the porcupine, for instance, an animal long bountied in my own state of Vermont. At first the successful hunter was expected to exhibit the animal to some local authority, such as the town clerk. This person solemnly viewed the remains and forked over the twenty-five cents. But porcupines may weigh thirty pounds apiece. If a man was eminently successful in the art of clubbing his share of porkies it would take a farm wagon to haul them to town. So it became the fashion to exhibit just the head, traditionally considered pretty good proof of death.

Just a head can get a little noisesome, however, on a hot August Saturday. Especially if you're not going to town until Tuesday. So the ante was reduced to just a pair of ears. After all, if you got close enough to one of these bark-eating, tree-girdling, dog-sticking critters to separate him from his ears, you must have got close enough to polish him off.

This worked fine. Porcupines have small, rounded hairy ears that are almost hidden by the coarse fur of the head. Each ear is less than the size of a dried apricot. Now you could put a whole day's worth of porcupines in your pocket.

Then somebody made an interesting discovery. With a deft hand and a few snips of the scissors, as many as a dozen pairs of "ears" could be cut from the belly skin of a single porky. So even if you'd had a slow day, all was not lost.

Or take the case of foxes. The display of the tail of a fox was bona fide evidence that you really had had the animal in hand, and the bounty was cheerfully paid.

You'd had him in hand, yes. But you didn't keep him long. Far better to turn him loose after you'd harvested his tail. Then he could raise six or eight fully-tailed youngsters for next year's crop.

There were further complications. Something had to be done with all those ears and tails. Often they went into a "bounty box," where they were supposed to be destroyed.

But somehow they occasionally found their way right back again for a second payment. Then, too, there was the brisk little trade in skins and ears and tails that developed across the border between a bounty-paying state and one that wasn't so enlightened.

The system was not favored unanimously, of course. Even in those days, long before man had seriously asked himself why there was such a wealth of wildlife if wolves and coyotes and bobcats were so destructive, questions were raised about the payments of bounties. But the clamor was endless, for man had not learned to live with the wild creatures around him. The records of the infant state of New York, two hundred years ago, bear witness to an argument on both sides. The resulting "varmint law," one of the oldest statutes of any kind on the books of the new United States of America, served as a model for other states. But it shortly gave rise to the term "bounty hunter," an epithet that implied you were a necessary evil, like paregoric or castor oil.

How well have the bounty hunters done their work? Or, put another way, how many less "varmints" are there now than before a price was put on their heads? Well, obviously there are fewer wolves. The bobcat bounty in Connecticut goes almost unclaimed, too, but it remains on the books—even if the sight of a single bobcat is front-page news anywhere in the state. Foxes are rarely seen. Golden eagles are nonexistent in our Eastern states; the remaining few are almost all confined to our Western back country.

All of these creatures would have dwindled in numbers as man tinkered with their habitat, anyway. And wildlife specialists have gathered plenty of evidence to the effect that bounties have seldom, if ever, accomplished the desired result. It is hard, though, to change the habits of three centuries—plus an Old World tradition where bounties have been in effect since before the time of Christ.

In my own state of Vermont, for example, the bounty on the porcupine was discontinued in 1954, at which time the porcupine had never been more plentiful. More than ten thousand dollars had been paid out for several years in a row before that, with no noticeable effect on total numbers. There were even more of the rambling rodents than there had been fifty years ago, in spite of a withering bounty over more than half the time.

It seems that the bounty, in the case of the porcupine, was like dipping water out of an overflowing tub instead of turning off the faucet. As the small family farm fell into disrepair with the general move to the city, the pastures and fields began to fill up with brush and saplings. Much of this was prime porcupine food. Then, too, the bobcat and "fisher-cat"—two effective enemies of the quill-pig—were hunted and trapped and bountied to the verge of extinction, themselves. The result was a porky explosion.

Now, belatedly, a contrite Vermont has imported several pairs of fishers from Maine. It has released these large dark-furred cousins of the mink at several areas. The fishers have gone to work at once. One ski area in northern Vermont has long budgeted two thousand dollars for porcupine damage per year. Now it finds itself with less than five hundred dollars' worth of repairs necessary to cabin siding, tool handles, tires and wiring. These were all former targets of the porky's passion for salt from sweaty hands, or just something to nibble on. "And last year we didn't really have any porcupine bills at all," the manager told me.

Or, since we're talking about coyotes, the experience of the state of Michigan speaks for itself. The heyday of bounties through the Midwest was in the 1930's and 1940's, when the fledgling science of wildlife management had hardly made itself known. From 1936 to 1946, payments were made on more than 23,000 coyotes. In the 1939–1940 fiscal year alone,

$36,000 was paid—at $15 per animal. But in spite of this un-flattering attention, coyotes got along better than ever. They were estimated to be half again as abundant at the end of the period as at the beginning.

Many wildlife men feel that a bounty may actually benefit a species. Especially a species like the coyote. It doesn't take the sagacious animal long to learn the dangers of traps, snares, poisoned carcasses—no matter how cleverly they are disguised. In fact, man's efforts at control may lead to a race of animals that is smarter than ever. The bungling ones get caught. For this reason many stockmen did not allow an inexperienced trapper on their lands: about all the trapper accomplished was to teach the coyotes what to avoid.

It was with the coming of the sheep, however, that the coyote found a new ally. The cattleman viewed the sheep and their masters with ill-concealed dismay. Those thousands of sharp, trampling hoofs carried creatures which cropped the grass down to the bare earth as no cattle had ever done on the open range. The ground over which sheep had grazed in those early days would often be little more than a dust bowl after they had passed. Indeed John Muir, the great naturalist, called the sheep "the hooved locust."

Into the middle of the dispute sprang the coyote. It could seldom catch and kill a calf, but a lamb was different; it could even kill a full-grown ewe. All that one lone coyote needed was to lure the shepherd's dog off to one side while its partner scattered the flock. Sometimes the coyote would even run over the backs of the terrified animals, sending them in all directions. Then, under cover of darkness, the two of them could pick off the stragglers.

This put the coyote in a different light from the standpoint of the cattlemen. They had suspected that he wasn't as bad as he had been painted—in cattle country, anyway. It was the feeling, and often the certainty, that the coyote more than paid for an occasional calf by keeping down the jackrabbits and mice and prairie dogs. These small animals, as the rancher could plainly see, were in direct competition with his cattle for the grass. So now the coyote actually walked the range with the cattleman's blessing.

The losses among the sheep were tragic; one account tells of more than a hundred of the animals killed in a night. And the coyote got the blame whether he deserved it or not. Another report tells of a flock so badly scattered that the shepherd never found more than half of them. A photograph given to me by an Idaho farmer shows four lambs, dead and scarcely eaten. Penciled on the back of the photo is the cryptic comment "we found 12 mor sheep in the gully."

Not all of the slaughter was the work of that howling, tireless little prairie wolf. In fact not even most of it. Every settlement had its dogs, and many of them had the freedom of the countryside. They banded together in packs, often being away from home for days at a time until finally they broke their ties with civilization altogether. They remain today, a threat to every living thing except man, roaming over the wilder parts of our country. As with the domestic cat gone wild, they combine an inborn cleverness with a lack of effective enemies to keep them in check. Thus they become a devastating menace.

I asked a biologist about those dogs. He spends much of his time in the California brush. "It is these wild dogs," he wrote, "that are responsible for the loss of thousands of animals a year, from the deer on down. And usually the coyote gets the credit. Not that he's scot-free, of course, but the deed is almost always laid at his door."

Whole communities, incensed at real or apparent coyote mischief, have taken arms at once. There have been mass raids on him, using everything from jeeps to aircraft in a big concerted drive. On more than one occasion these drives have backfired—as in one Southwest vendetta where every coyote was killed in an effort to improve the quail population. But the embarrassed hunters had to reverse their field and actually put the coyote on the protected list. After they got rid of him there were fewer quail than ever. It seems that a main item of coyote diet was the cotton rat, a mortal enemy of the ground-nesting quail.

Today a good part of the "control" of the coyote—and cotton rats and other animals in man's disfavor—is vested in a new type of bounty-seeker: the "government hunter." His bounty is in the wages he's paid out of United States Fish and Wildlife Service funds. In the name of "varmint control," in the past he has tossed poisoned bait out of airplanes, sending untold victims to agonizing deaths. As a government-paid agent, his interest is, predictably, in results. Short-term, that is. The incredibly delicate balance of ecology seldom enters into it.

At times there have been as many as six hundred of these predator-control agents operating in the field at once, earning a living, as a pamphlet in the mail recently informed me, "in the Great Outdoors, where you live a wonderful life close to Nature."

But *what* a Nature!—no coyotes calling, no bark of a prairie dog, no squall of a bobcat. The last wolverine dying because it ate the raven that ate the snake that ate the mouse that ate the grain coated with that almost indestructible poison, 1080. This rodenticide—technically, sodium fluoroacetate—is so long-lasting that it affects a whole chain of living things beyond the mouse it was intended to control. A Nature indeed, carefully fashioned according to Orders from Headquarters and which, tragically, might find its complexion changed after a given national election.

But Don Coyote has survived the curses and threats and vituperations heaped on him by an ungrateful populace. He continues to widen his range. Now it covers the western half of the United States and Canada, stretching along the northern states, Quebec and Ontario to Maine. It goes down through Mexico, too. Although I have never been able to get a wildlife man to commit himself, most estimates say the coyote is more than a million strong.

The coyote has been shipped to Alaska for breeding with sled dogs. A clever pet if taken young enough, he's been hauled off to Florida. He has escaped in both places. Now his descendants seek their fortunes in the home of their ancestors, for coyotes apparently once roamed over almost the entire continent. They have long set up housekeeping just outside rural towns and hamlets, reaping any fringe benefits that might present themselves.

If a man sets a trap for them, they soon learn to avoid it—even if the trap has been buried in a manure pit to kill any human smell and is covered with debris so it doesn't show. The coyote disdainfully uncovers the trap or throws gravel at it until it snaps. Or, in that supreme gesture of contempt, it sprinkles the trap with a well-directed spray of urine.

Occasionally you hear of Old Peg-Leg, or One-Eye or Three-Toes. Nearly always this animal turns out to have lost a part of its anatomy in a close call with man. Now it is doubly cautious, and a bigger headache than ever to the farmer. Not only has it gained wisdom through bitter experience, but its handicap has forced it to prey on the easy pickings afforded by sheep and poultry and barnyard pets.

In happier times, however, the *coyotl*, as the Aztecs knew him, goes along minding his own business. This naturally consists of snooping into the business of every rat and rabbit within a three-mile circle, with perhaps a side order of prickly pear fruit for variety. If a traveler jogs through his territory, the coyote will watch from a distance, and then go down to sniff the stranger's track.

If the traveler happens to stop for the night in a two-wheeled contraption or a flimsy canvas shelter, that's all right, too: the coyote lifts his nose to the sky and serenades the intruder from the military crest of a nearby hill.

And the traveler shivers a bit, and sees things in his Coleman lantern—and is much the richer for the rest of his life because of the bounty system that failed to work.